Youth Ministry
After the Pandemic

Youth Ministry After the Pandemic

A Practical Theology from the Global South

KEVIN MURIITHI NDEREBA

Foreword by Shantelle Weber

WIPF & STOCK · Eugene, Oregon

YOUTH MINISTRY AFTER THE PANDEMIC
A Practical Theology from the Global South

Copyright © 2025 Kevin Muriithi Ndereba. All rights reserved. Except for brief quotations in critical publications or reviews, no part of this book may be reproduced in any manner without prior written permission from the publisher. Write: Permissions, Wipf and Stock Publishers, 199 W. 8th Ave., Suite 3, Eugene, OR 97401.

Wipf & Stock
An Imprint of Wipf and Stock Publishers
199 W. 8th Ave., Suite 3
Eugene, OR 97401

www.wipfandstock.com

PAPERBACK ISBN: 978-1-6667-5659-3
HARDCOVER ISBN: 978-1-6667-5660-9
EBOOK ISBN: 978-1-6667-5661-6

VERSION NUMBER 07/21/25

Unless otherwise indicated, all Scripture quotations are from the ESV® Bible (The Holy Bible, English Standard Version®), Copyright © 2001 by Crossway Bibles, a publishing ministry of Good News Publishers. Used by permission. All rights reserved.

Chapter 5 reproduced with permission from *Acta Theologica*

Chapter 6 reproduced with permission from *Palgrave Global Handbook for Social Change*

Chapter 8 reproduced with permission from *Zygon*

I dedicate this book to the many youth workers in Africa
who serve by faith and not by sight.
May their labors bear much fruit for the kingdom.

A special dedication to my wife Jessica, who has stood with me
in my ministry to youth and as I spent time writing.

Contents

Lists of Illustrations or Tables | viii
Foreword by Shantelle Weber | ix
Acknowledgments | xi
Abbreviations | xiii

1. Envisioning a Global Portrait | 1
2. Practicing Global Youth Faith Formation | 9
3. Honoring the Community | 27
4. Considering the Power of Music | 36
5. Navigating iGens and Digital Church | 42
6. Caring for Young People After the Pandemic | 55
7. Nurturing a Politically-Engaged Faith | 74
8. Understanding Youth Leaving Faith for Science | 90
9. Raising Youth Ecotheologians | 114
10. Advocating for Youth and Economic Justice | 131
11. Peering into the Promising Future | 139

Bibliography | 143

Lists of Illustrations or Tables

Figure 1: Youth Cohorts Served by the PCEA Church | 63

Figure 2: Size of the PCEA Youth Ministries in Local Churches | 64

Figure 3: Emerging Youth Issues in Light of the COVID-19 Pandemic | 65

Figure 4: Diagram Showing Science-Religion Overlap | 109

Figure 5: The Practical Theology Cycle | 133

Table 1: Summary of Findings from Youth Survey on Non-Religion | 95–98

Table 2: Summary of Findings from Youth Survey on Ecotheology | 122–23

Foreword

IT IS AN HONOR writing this foreword to acknowledge the work of a colleague and pastor in youth ministry in Kenya. Writing as a practical theologian from an evangelical Reformed perspective, I appreciate his intersection of congregational youth ministry and young people serving as public theologians beyond the walls of institutional churches. I also appreciate the auto-ethnographic approach to his writing, which Ndebera seems to embrace by taking us as readers into the heart of the Kenyan people.

Ndereba introduces the reader to the context of Kenya as it connects to envisioning a global portrait. He highlights how the role of young people in the political process largely mirrors their role within ecclesiastical life but sadly remains isolated within both these spaces. He notes, however, that the same young people are the ones driving real change and progress within the corporate space despite various constraints of life.

This book moves the concept of faith formation from a dichotomized, spiritualized, and privatized vision of faith, to a transformed and transforming faith participating in the discourses of the church, society, and academy. For long-lasting faith among young people, faith formation must not stand isolated from but must discerningly engage the complex landscape of African youth cultures and subcultures, intellectually and affectively.

The core distinction of this work lies in chapters 3 and 4 where Ndereba honors the role of African community in African scholarship and contextually-based, faith-formation practice by integrating the centrality of song as an African language and way of life. Such a communal reading of how faith is formed is different from an individualistic conception that truncates holistic development of young people. African youth and church are not separated from the digital world of fast-paced technological advances. *Youth Ministry After the Pandemic* acknowledges this in how we relate to, offer pastoral care for, and disciple young people. Churches have for too long ignored the impact of global politics on our worldviews and life choices. Young people have spotlighted these and forced the church to engage in theologies that faithfully disciple them, theologies that critically reflect science, ecology, justice, and the meanings of these for young people navigating their faith journeys.

I would agree with Ndebera that this book is the first of its kind on this continent. It is a holistic account of youth culture in Africa at the intersection of church, faith, and public life as Africans engage with the rest of the world. It is also an example of how international networks and scholarship can be shared contextually. *Youth Ministry After the Pandemic* calls the church towards intentional youth discipleship that engages these youth as the church.

    Shantelle Weber
    Associate Professor, Practical Theology
    Faculty of Theology, Stellenbosch University
    President of the International Association
        for the Study of Youth Ministry

Acknowledgments

I AM GRATEFUL TO God for the adventurous journey he has taken me in serving young people and writing with/about them. I have learned much from them that has shaped my ministry and my academic work as a practical theologian.

Along the way, I have met a band of ministers and scholars who share a similar passion for young people, mostly through the International Association for the Study of Youth Ministry (IASYM). They include my African colleagues and professors Nathan, Seyram, Garth, "Reggie," Nene, Shantelle, and Anita, as well as the other colleagues and professors with whom we have served in the international board, including Graham, Amy, Beth, "Gretch," Gareth, Frantisek, Monique, Scott, Joyson, and Christian. Thank you for your holy passions towards young people and your vocational friendship. Fellow youth workers in the National Association of Youth Workers Network (NAYNET) in Kenya have been sojourners and supporters in my research work. They opened me up to diverse voices of young people who feature prominently in this book. These young people truly give important insight for how the church in Africa can lead, not only in navigating the diverse spiritual landscapes of the continent but also in shaping a publicly-engaged faith. I am indebted to their critiques, contributions, and thoughtful ideas.

Special acknowledgement goes to Rev. Dr. Edward Buri, who was my youth pastor of many years before his ordination as a minister of word and sacrament in the Presbyterian Church of East Africa (PCEA). He models the sort of intellectual and pastoral sensitivity in his vocation as a minister that has been a model for youth ministry in Kenya. He carries the concern and advocacy for young people of the church father, the late Very

Acknowledgments

Rev. Dr. George Wanjau (who was parish minister in my home parish of St. Andrew's and past moderator of the General Assembly). Rev. Wanjau's rich legacy of ministry in the PCEA and in ecumenical circles speak on his behalf even beyond his earthly journey.

Several institutions are also important for the contents of this book. St. Paul's University has provided an academic home for me, and I am grateful for my colleagues in the School of Theology, led by the dean of the school Dr. Julius Kithinji. The Global Reformed Advocacy Platforms for Engagement (GRAPE), hosted by the Rev. Drs. Claudia and Dirk Haarmann through the World Communion of Reformed Churches (WCRC), immersed me in the practical work of advocacy, modelling the important role of the church in public engagement. This work has helped me to link youth work and its public facing significance—youth as public theologians, as I hope this book shows in some places.

This book captures some of my work during my doctoral dissertation at the University of South Africa under Professor Garth Aziz, as well as additional research that I have undertaken since. A constant figure throughout has been my dear wife and adventure partner, my dear Jessica. Thank you for your generosity of support and understanding.

Abbreviations

AACC—All Africa Conference of Churches

ACMS—Anglican Church Missionary Society

AU—Africa Union

BIG—The Basic Income Grant

CCM—Contemporary Christian Music

CST—Catholic Social Teaching

EAK—Evangelical Alliance of Kenya

EBCOSA—Evangelical Bible Church of Southern Africa

EPRI—Economic Policy Research Institute

FOCUS—Fellowship of Christian Unions

GRAPE—Global Reformed Advocacy Platforms for Engagement

IASYM—The International Association for the Study of Youth Ministry

IFES—International Fellowship of Evangelical Students

INSBSS—International Research Network for the Study of Belief and Science in Society

ISSSC—Institute for the Study of Secularism in Society and Culture

JYT—*Journal of Youth and Theology*

KYDP—Kenya Youth Development Policy

KYFC—Kenya Youth for Christ

MTD—Moralistic Therapeutic Deism

Abbreviations

NAYNET—National Youth Workers Network

NCCK—National Council of Churches of Kenya

NSRN—International Nonreligion and Secularity Research Network

NSYR—National Study for Youth and Religion

PCEA—Presbyterian Church of East Africa

SSA—Sub-Saharan Africa

UN—United Nations

WCF—*Westminster Confession of Faith*

WCRC—World Communion of Reformed Churches

1

Envisioning a Global Portrait

NESTLED IN THE EASTERN region of the African continent, the city Nairobi has affectionately been described as "the city under the sun." Housing important international organizations such as the United Nations (UN) and World Bank, Kenya is a significant contributor not only to the economic life of the region but also to the technological design and global uptake of software and mobile money solutions. A drive across the country will take you to the highest point, Mt. Kenya, or across sprawling green ranches and national parks, across the sandy coastal region, or maybe the semi-desert of the northern region, and if you are lucky enough, you may come face-to-face with one of the Big Five.

Despite these colorful images of the country, there is a way in which Christianity, which has the lion's share of religious identities in the country, has a complex relationship with the state. The same country that experienced democratic reforms in the late 1980s and early 1990s, largely due to the role of influential ecclesiastical figures such as Timothy Njoya and Henry Okullu, is the same country where people from their two ethnicities (Kikuyu and Luo) and others clashed in the 2007–2008 post-election violence, largely blind to their mutual faith but more irritated by their ethnic background. Perhaps no other African country like Rwanda shares this complex narrative of negative ethnicity.[1] The 2012 and 2017 Kenyan elections stemmed the tide of this dialectic.

1. Longman, *Christianity and Genocide*.

Political provocations aside, the role of young people in the political process largely mirrors their role within ecclesiastical life. Characterized by an equal dose of doubt and disillusionment, young people remain isolated within both political and ecclesiastical spaces. Both spaces navigate a parochial attitude towards "youth," worsened within African cultures and societies with very high-power distance. Yet within corporate spaces, these same young people are the ones driving real change and progress, often within various constraints of life. This book isn't about politics. Yet, it is about the lives of young people often navigating various sociopolitical contexts and turmoil.

In the wake of the COVID pandemic, the task of youth ministry cannot be ignored. Given the high levels of mobilities and migrations, ideas and people travel just as fast and in equal measure. Theological reflection is either playing catch-up or trying to match the exuberance and complexities that globalization brings. Within the classical sense, beyond the golden years of theology as queen of the sciences, the enlightenment era has powerfully relegated theology as a discipline on the margins. This type of thinking traps theological reflection within the domains of systematic reflection of doctrine, exegetical complexities of language, and "pure" practical ministry, oftentimes bereft of the "poisonous" role of theological depth. Yet in a global age of various transitions and transformations, theological reflection that can bridge the divides is needed. Theological reflection that takes very seriously the theories and praxis involved in the engagement of the world's young people is sorely needed.

WHAT THIS BOOK IS ABOUT

This book is about youth ministry. But it is not about traditional youth ministry. By "traditional youth ministry," I mean narrowly focused academic reflection on youth ministry that foregrounds voices, contexts, topics, and cultures from the West. Rather, this book contends that in the context of global Christianity, voices, contexts, topics, and cultures of the Global South also have a seat at the table. It is in light of such an expansive table that we share the rich textures and tastes from our diverse and shared Christian life. A second issue that adds to the positionality of this book is the post-COVID reality of the merging of the digital with lived realities, and all the transformations that this has brought. This includes issues to do with belonging and community and interaction with the emerging field of digital ecclesiology, the contemporary practice of pastoral care, as well as the prospects and challenges surrounding missiology to the next generations in Africa. Finally, by public theology, this book moves the concept of faith formation from a dichotomized, spiritualized, and privatized vision of faith, to a transformed and faith that participates in the discourses of the church, society, and academy.

This book does not ignore the place of academic and contextual reflection of youth ministry from the Western Hemisphere. Instead, it views these within unique Christian perspectives that are aware of global discourses in the theological terrain. This book casts a bird's eye view of various topics, perspectives, themes, and approaches all from within a global Christian perspective. Much of the existing scholarship of youth ministry, particularly monographs and edited books, originates from within or is written sorely for the North American and Western context. To its praise, this has deepened the significance of academic reflection of youth ministry, moving it beyond an appendage to real theological reflection or a hodgepodge of entertaining candy that is soft on the inside and does not amount to much, and toward a noteworthy enterprise in the theological guild. Following the call of key scholars in youth ministry such as Root and Dean, this book fits the mold of sustained theological reflection on Christian ministry to young people, not merely as pawns in a chess game but imagers of and co-agents with God who are worthy of careful attention; and as God's garden, worthy of tending.[2] This book takes this call seriously and casts it within the multi-veined arms of global Christianity. As Escobar eloquently says as he summarizes the story of a young Spaniard, José Antonio Gonzalez, who emigrated from his hometown in Galicia, Spain, to Germany and was converted through the gospel ministry of Mrs. Pinto, an immigrant Bolivian housewife: "Christian mission in the twenty-first century has become the responsibility of the global church." Both in Germany and in Kenya, as well as other parts of the world, young people are so central to the story of global Christianity.[3]

Yet if one considers the state of the field in practical theology, and particularly youth ministry, there is an abundance of resources that fit this mold. What sets this book apart? In addition to offering a theological reflection on youth ministry, this book explores this task within the scope of global Christianity. Global Christianity tells the revolutionary story of how the Christian faith is not home to any one culture but is always in

---

2. Root and Dean, *Theological Turn*, 19.
3. Escobar, *Time for Mission*, 1.

transition—or to use Lamin Sanneh's specific terminology: in "translation"—meaning that the Christian story navigates cultures, contexts, and continents.[4] Scholars have continued to formulate, reformulate, and critique this thesis of the gravity of the Christian narrative as tethered to the Global South.[5] What is beyond a shadow of doubt is that the Global South is emerging in its contribution to the global Christian discourse—not only quantitatively but also qualitatively.

Quantitatively, consider the growth of the Christian movement in the Global South. Jenkins's thesis of the growth of global Christianity to the Southern Hemisphere merely popularized the statistics collated by David Barrett in 1982 in his *World Christian Encyclopedia*, which was an expansion of the five editions (1949–1968) of the *World Christian Handbook*.[6] In it, he observed the remarkable growth of Christianity in Asia, Africa, Oceania, and Latin America, tracing that growth from 1900. Christians in the Global South in 1900 only comprised 18 percent, compared with 82 percent in the Global North.[7] By 2020, Zurlo, Johnson, and Crossing observe that Christians in the Global South comprised 67 percent with 667 million Christians in Africa, 612 million in Latin America, and 379 million in Asia, compared to 565 million in Europe and 268 million in North America.[8] According to them, the projected growth of Christianity in the Global South by 2050 is estimated to be 77 percent of the global Christian population. Some correlate this palpable growth with the high birth rates in Africa and the conversion of people from other religions in countries like Mongolia, Cambodia, India, and elsewhere in Asia.[9] While this comparative growth of Christianity in the Global South and the decline of Christianity in the Global North is fairly known in the academy, much of its implication awaits theological reflection in the field of youth ministry.

Qualitatively, there is a growing body of research on youth ministry in the African context, and the Asian context is closely following. Consider also that Africa and Asia are two of the youngest continents in terms of demographics in the world. This means that theological reflection on this critical demographic is key for the advance of Christian mission as well as

4. Sanneh, *Translating the Message*.
5. Jenkins, *Next Christendom*.
6. Zurlo et al., "World Christianity and Mission," 8.
7. Zurlo et al., "World Christianity and Mission," 9.
8. Zurlo et al., "World Christianity and Mission," 10.
9. Hackett and Stonawski, "Changing Global Religious Landscape."

the decolonization of theological education in a manner that attends to a variety of widening concerns and focus areas in research agenda.[10] A notable presence is the International Association for the Study of Youth Ministry (IASYM), which brings together academics and practitioners around the theme of youth ministry. Their *Journal of Youth and Theology* remains a critical voice in the academic reflection of youth ministry, and there is a growing presence of emerging global voices on the various tasks, methodologies, models, practices, approaches, and theories on youth ministry. Key voices from the South African context include Garth Aziz, Reggie Nel, Anita Cloete, and Shantelle Weber. These colleagues have significantly engaged the complexities involved in the South African context, including the history of apartheid, decolonization of education, technological advance, and faith formation. In the East African context, Nathan Chiroma (who also writes for his West African, Nigerian context) and I have contributed significant knowledge in the areas of theological education, mentorship, and apologetics ministry and methodology. Significant room remains in the western and northern regions of Africa.

While noting both the quantitative and qualitative growth of Christian reflection on youth ministry, particularly in Africa, this book aims at locking arms with other global voices. In significant ways, this book seeks to offer a truly "ecumenical spirit." Noting the landmark World Missionary Conference of 1910 in Edinburgh, this book serves as a conference of ideas, yet expanding on the concept of "ecumenical" that was ironically absent in that landmark gathering.[11] I use "ecumenical" in the old sense of the word, as in "ecumenical councils," where the different Christian traditions are seen as streams of thinking that help us to rally around "essential Christianity." Appreciating that there are limits and boundaries, I have limited the breadth of traditions to within what I would call "evangelical and ecumenical."

THE BOOK'S THEOLOGICAL PERSPECTIVE

This is certainly important to the book's readers, particularly when one observes the marker "evangelical" within the North American context. Given the US Democrat and Republican contentions surrounding race and power, one appreciates how this Christian marker of identity has been used to support injustices of various stripes. By broadly "evangelical," I refer to the

---

10. Weber, "Decolonising Youth Ministry," 10.
11. Stanley, "World Missionary Conference," 330.

kind of theology that is centered on the person and work of Jesus Christ, that engages the word of God from a confessional standpoint, that focuses on a personal relationship with God, and that emphasizes the Spirit's work in accomplishing God's mission within the difficult situations of our world (as you can see from the book's themes).[12] Whereas I am sympathetic to the way that this identity marker of "evangelical" has been negatively used in the North American context to support American nationalism, racism, and other systemic issues, the researcher uses it here in the traditional sense that it has been used.[13]

Additionally, since practical theology is always sensitive to the researcher's positionality, I also approach many of the topics in this book from the Reformed tradition. This will be very clear in the discussion on digital ecclesiology, where I use concepts from Reformed theology in the work of Berkhoff and the Westminster Standards. While criticisms to this theological tradition can be made from the vantage point of the evangelical criticisms, I acknowledge the growing need to challenge hegemonic emphases from our theological positions and to engage critically and contextually with the issues that these theologies encounter with, in this case, African realities. I am, for example, sympathetic to how this tradition has been sympathetic to the race and justice dialogue, particularly within the history of the Reformed churches in South Africa through the initial encounters with Dutch Calvinists, French Huguenots, and later by the Scottish Presbyterians and Swiss missionaries.[14] Tshaka here raises the importance of theological approaches that are always in "interlocution," not only with contexts of the margins but also theologies from the margins.

What this means for the case of global Christianity, for example, is an engagement with Pentecostal theologies. Doing this may not only lead to a heightened sense of self-understanding but also a sense of charity that enlarges one's theological vision while also sensitively critiquing particular discontents and malpractices that arise from extremes in both Reformed and Pentecostal theologies. If we laud the rise of Christianity in the Global South at all, the reality is that this type of Christianity is indigenous and Pentecostal in orientation. On the surface level, Reformed theologians usually want to characterize all Pentecostal orientations as "excessive," which would be similar to characterizing all Reformed theology as only

12. Wells, *No Place for Truth*, 5–6.
13. Larsen and Daniel, *Cambridge Companion*, 10.
14. Tshaka, "African and Reformed," 4.

"hyper-Calvinist." The reality is that there are different shades and stripes of Reformed theology. A case in point is the Presbyterian make-up in the West, where one has the Dutch Calvinistic streams, "orthodox" Presbyterianism, as well as "liberal" Presbyterianism in the United States. Similarly, in Kenya one has a small minority of Reformed Baptists, as well as more confessional expressions of Reformed Presbyterianism, among others—in fact, the "charismatization" of mainstream churches in Africa has led to interesting expressions of Presbyterianism that are more Pentecostal in orientation. All this is to say that acknowledging one's positionality is important for theological engagement. This book therefore peers into the subdiscipline from these orientations, aware that there are many other towers that give different and even stellar views.

PUTIN AND A PANORAMIC VIEW OF YOUTH MINISTRY

This book is about publicly engaged youth ministry. And youth are a critical demographic for any society concerned about the current global affairs or the future promises of restorative justice. While continents such as Africa and Asia are made up of youthful populations, theological reflections have not correlated to this promising trend. Yet, within popular cultures and societies, young people are playing crucial roles in corporate leadership, governance, media, and arts industries, and usually doing so in an encouraging way. Is the church and Christian academy behind? One may consider perhaps the actor Lupita Nyong'o, a contribution of the East African country to the global stage of cinema. Corporate business rooms are also filled with young men and women of promise, bringing turnarounds within various sectors. With the exceptions of a few urban churches in Kenya's cities and towns, many elder sessions and vestries are missing in age representation of young people. Conversations in theological institutions are still grappling with issues of a bygone era, rather than engaging contextual realities facing the next generations. I ask again, is the church and Christian academy behind? What might theological reflection as well as ministry engagement portend for these young people at the margins of African societies? Are there theological articulations that can serve the concerns, questions, and longings of the young people around us? While I do not argue here for age segregation, as if the younger or older counterparts are monochromatic, there is a need for including young people within the church's vision. I have persuasively advocated for youth inclusivity within ecclesial spaces, noting its theological and cultural challenges, and how this can be done, especially within mainstream contexts.[15] A notable book project has also developed theologies for children engagement in Africa.[16] These are examples of enhancing youth agency in the lives of religious communities and in public life.

At the time of writing this book (May 2025), I am aware of the global politics happening in Ukraine, and the confluence of political power, racism, and religion that are often intertwined in vicious ways. These vicious cycles of sociopolitical fragmentation are not constrained to post-secular Europe but are also presently tangible in Nigeria and the United States—a nation reeling from recent murders and gun-violence directed towards school-going children and elderly men and women by the hands of disenfranchised youth. These disenfranchised youth may share different skin color with those whose hands were stained in blood in my own Kenyan context of the 2007–2008 post-election violence, but they share their energy, their promises, and their perils. Within the same vein, we are in the wake of another vicious cycle in the past two years of the global COVID pandemic. Yet in the dark moments of the coronavirus, young people were at the forefront of designing new spaces of worship, education, business, and technological mobility. These young people are what this book is about. This book is about bringing key global voices at the table of theological reflection—those with the best tools of practical theology, sociology, systematic theology, biblical exegesis, inter-cultural sensitivity, and pastoral wisdom—to the explorations of the daily lived realities of young people all over the world and the attendant opportunity for building bridges between the theory and practices of youth and African Christianity.

These chapters present the case of youth ministry as a global task of not only spiritual formation that also presents as an opportunity for public transformation in the light of the challenges of globalization. In a shrinking world, ever so smaller within the digital and "post-COVID" reality, there is a need for envisaging youth ministry within a wider and global scope of theological reflection. This approach is engaged and strengthened by attentive sociological research, biblical exegesis, and the sociopolitical contexts of worldview clashes, political turmoil, post-colonial realities, and digital interconnection that enriches scholars within the fields of discussion in their work with and among today's most abandoned and most promising demographic—young people.

15. Ndereba, "Let Them Come."
16. Grobbelaar and Breed, *Welcoming Africa's Children*.

2

Practicing Global Youth Faith Formation

Young people comprise a majority of Africa's population, yet youth in Africa are under-theorized within the theological literature, particularly within the contemporary conversation in African theology and African Christianity. With the critical awareness of Christianity as a global faith, there is need to theoretically engage with the largest population of people in the continent and in the Christian demographic. While there is a lively engagement within the field of practical theology of Africa's youth, there are few theological resources that help churches nurture the faith of young people in a holistic way. Faith formation of young people in Africa is viewed from various perspectives. One view engages the task of faith formation merely as anxiety-ridden evangelistic witnessing, with a primary aim of conversion. Another view outsources the long-term process of faith formation to pastoral leaders in churches, with a truncated view of the architecture of communities that includes the family or schooling system; these are viewed as either an aid or hinderance to holistic faith formation.

On the other extreme, church governance in different denominations can often skew the leadership development of young people based on various factors. In the mission churches, leaders can be overly invested in maintaining the church's structures rather than engaging in visionary ministry that can catapult a new generation forward into God's grand mission. Among the newer charismatic and some independent churches that have littered the ecclesiological landscape of this vibrant continent, church leadership is often the preserve of a "mum" or "dad," with attendant political control to ensure the mileage of the visionary's agenda.[1] Needless to say, there are several iterations on both these groups of churches in the African continent. The point is that church leaders can sometimes be sidetracked from the calling of forming the faith of a generation undergoing massive cultural upheavals because of the sociopolitical undercurrents that are a part of shepherding any community of faith.

Given these constraints, churches are sometimes challenged when it comes to not only reaching out to young people but also nurturing the faith of new converts in rapidly transforming urban African contexts. Intercultural and worldview engagement, adolescent development, and vocational discernment are a few issues that such faith nurturing efforts are called to respond to in a cosmopolitan African context. This chapter argues that an integrative model of faith formation is crucial for holistic development of young people. It utilizes an evangelical theological framework and engages key scholars in theology, anthropology, and human development to contextualize faith formation or discipleship of young people in African cities. More specifically, this chapter supports the book's argument that in order to nurture a long-lasting faith among young people, faith formation must not stand isolated, but must discerningly engage the complex landscape of African youth cultures and subcultures, both intellectually and effectively.

In the past decade, the "youth bulge" has been used as an adjective in describing the African continent. It has been proposed by and utilized within socioeconomic literature in view of creating more youth-inclusive societies. Theological reflection is thereby a critical tool that can safeguard the future of the African societies within which churches and faith communities operate. If churches can nurture young people who are characterized by a robust faith, then African growth and development can be sustained in the long run. Much more, these young people are the same ones who will usher in the African nations and ethnicities into eschatological glory, as per the apostolic witness. With the growing numbers of young people, theological reflection on youth issues is pertinent. The academic exploration of youth studies has been approached from economic, social science, psychological, and philosophical perspectives, and though this has born significant fruit, this book orients the topic within the discipline of practical theology. Practical theological reflection takes into consideration the

---

1. "Mum" and "dad" are terms used to refer to spiritual leaders in charismatic and Pentecostal churches.

lived experiences of faith communities—in this case, young people. The choice of practical theology is based on its interdisciplinary nature, which enriches theological reflection by engaging the insights of other disciplines.

LISTENING TO THE CHORUS OF FAITH FORMATION

One of the subject areas in the practical theological reflection of youth ministry is faith or spiritual formation, which in this book is considered synonymously. What differentiates other types of youth work and Christian youth work or youth ministry is the faith formation aspect. Yet since young people in Africa navigate complex sociopolitical situations, economic challenges, multi-cultural frameworks, as well as plural religious identities, faith formation of young people must be engaged in a reflexive manner—both traversing the theoretical underpinnings of youth ministry as well as the practical skills and knowledge bases for effective work with young people. Youth malformation in this book is described as the complexities surrounding the spiritual identification of young people, the difficulty in churches engaging and retaining young people, as well as the missiological challenges from secular worldviews and entities that confront the church. As such, this book generally engages current empirical studies in youth faith formation, theories on adolescent growth and development, as well as emerging adulthood. In particular, this book explores how youth cultures and subcultures in a postmodern and postcolonial African context influence faith formation of young people, as envisioned in the preceding statements.

Most of the resources on the faith formation of next generations are written from within and for a largely Western context. Ross Stuart-Buttle and John Shortt, for example, focus on Christian education, particularly in the educational contexts of European and North American countries.[2] Anne E. Streaty Wimberly and Evelyn L. Parker engage the topic of faith formation through the insights of pan-African scholars, primarily writing within the framework of religious education for the African American and North American environment.[3] Steve Emery-Wright and Ed Mackenzie's work is important in its proposal of a networks approach to faith formation.[4] The beneficence of this latter proposal is that it views the task of faith formation through the lens of community. Chap Clark argues in the same

---

2. Stuart-Buttle and Shortt, *Christian Faith*.
3. Wimberly and Parker, *In Search of Wisdom*.
4. Emery-Wright and Mackenzie, *Networks for Faith Formation*.

light when he talks of "adoptive faith."[5] In other words, the task of faith formation is not the reserve of one individual or one group but that of the entire network of people and groupings that surround young people. Christian Smith's and Melina Lundquist Denton's research in the National Study for Youth and Religion (NSYR) has been foundational as a qualitative study on the religious landscape of young people in America.[6] Together with Kenda Creasy Dean, their theorizing of Moralistic Therapeutic Deism (MTD) as the theological framework of adolescents has been a launching pad for multidisciplinary reflections on young people and religion.[7] What emerges from the research is how the descriptors of the faith of young people are correlated, either positively or negatively, with descriptors of the faith of adults in the communities of faith.[8] According to their research, MTD describes how American teenagers view God or the Christian faith:

- as "moralistic" meaning, a legalistic approach to faith with a list of rights and wrongs;
- as "therapeutic" meaning, God is there for their self-improvement, self-fulfillment, and self-actualization;
- as "deistic" meaning, God is far removed from everyday affairs and can be put on like "Sunday-best" clothes on one day of the week.[9]

Andrew Root has been slightly critical of this MTD shibboleth in youth ministry scholarship, noting that despite its helpfulness, it is a contemporary sociocultural descriptor rather than something anchored in the church's discussion of faith formation in its historical development.[10] A central approach that the church has used in forming the faith of a myriad of believers through the centuries has been through its creeds and confessions, which not only help them respond to various "malformations" but also teach Christians how to think and live.[11] Root engages Charles Taylor's insights on secularization by noting that the church's obsession with youthfulness rests on the sociocultural and historical antecedents of the North

---

5. Clark, *Adoptive Youth Ministry*.
6. Smith and Denton, *Soul Searching*.
7. Dean, *Almost Christian*.
8. Dean, *Almost Christian*, 18.
9. Dean, *Almost Christian*, 163–64.
10. Root, *Faith Formation*, xvii.
11. Kapic, "Systematic Theology."

American youth movement as opposed to a biblical and theologically coherent framework.[12] For faith to last, young people must be connected to a community that has a consistent identity—in this context, communities that are defined by the indelible marks of adoption and what that means for their day to day living and aspirations. This, it seems, is the only antidote against cheap caricatures of faith.

David Setran and Chris Kiesling also engage the task of spiritual formation in light of the developing theory in the area of "emerging adulthood."[13] This theory of emerging adulthood seeks to understand the unique generational markers that distinguish one cohort of young people from similar cohorts in the past.[14] Scholars in emerging adulthood, for example, have looked at shifts in digital media consumption and production, the age of getting married and beginning families, and the growing complexities in vocational discernment, all of which are leading to an extension of the adolescent years beyond the late teens into the mid-twenties. These scholars understand emerging adulthood as a phase that is distinct from adolescence and young adulthood, while others see continuities between them. Whichever way one understands it, young adults are taking longer to settle into traditional adult roles in society such as vocational direction, family life, and societal service among others. In several African countries, the mean age of marriage has been rising over the years, with marked differences in rural and urban areas. In Kenya, for example, women in the 1940s were married when they were eighteen years old on average, whereas in 2015 the average age was over twenty-two years old in Nairobi among women aged from twenty-five to forty-nine years old, and over twenty-six years old among men aged from thirty to fifty-four years old.[15] Other changing patterns are in the area of cohabitation as an accepted social norm and drastic changes in teenage relationships within the COVID pandemic in the areas of gender and sexual violence, early pregnancies, and increasing transactional relationships.[16] The implications for these insights to faith formation are numerous.

Evidently, literature on faith formation is not malnourished. The lacuna is in whether these theories can adequately engage youth urban

---

12. Root, *Faith Formation*, 13.
13. Setran and Kiesling, *Spiritual Formation*.
14. Arnett and Hughes, *Adolescence and Emerging Adulthood*.
15. Pike et al., "Making Sense of Marriage," 1299.
16. Karp et al., "Youth Relationships," 754.

contexts in Africa. Such contexts have vestiges of industrialization while still grappling with underdevelopment in various aspects. Although these books make important arguments, they lack the contextual engagement with issues within the African context. What appears in the African continent are disparate articles that engage the issue of youth faith formation.[17] To my knowledge, only two books on the continent tackle the issue of faith formation. Malan Nel, the don of youth ministry scholarship, has published a book on youth ministry in 2018, arguing for an "inclusive missional approach."[18] However, the book is more general in its subject matter as it deals with many important topics in youth ministry. The other book, which tackles faith formation in a roundabout fashion, is by Anita Cloete.[19] The strength of her book is its multidisciplinary perspectives, yet its scope is narrowed to media and religion. Thus, this book is unique in that it brings the theories in adolescent development and faith formation in dialogue with sociocultural issues within the framework of theological reflection and focused on the local church.

From a global perspective, several studies on the faith formation of young people have been conducted. Weber lists four studies, citing the first study as Smith and Denton conducted between 2001 and 2005, focusing on adolescents between thirteen and seventeen years of age.[20] The second study she cites is by Powell, Griffin, and Crawford who longitudinally surveyed five hundred youth pastors from 2004 to 2010. Third is a quantitative study by Pieterse, Van der Ven, and Dreyer from Dutch and South African universities through two surveys (1995–1996 and 2000–2002) in the same selected schools in the Pretoria and Johannesburg areas. The fourth study is by Shantelle Weber who conducted a research study in 2008 and 2012 in order to understand youth faith formation among fourteen- to seventeen-year-olds in eight local congregations in South Africa. The fifth is a three-year study by Osmer and Douglass of more than three thousand North American congregations across five denominations, including seven thousand parents, youth, and leaders that explored the practice of confirmation as faith formation.[21] My doctoral work also focused on faith formation among fifteen young

---

17. Avenant et al., "Intergenerational Faith Formation"; Ndereba, "Ubuntu Apologetics"; Counted, "Psychology of Youth"; Weber, "Formation of Young People."

18. Nel, *Youth Ministry*.

19. Cloete, *Interdisciplinary Reflections*.

20. Weber, "(South) African Voice."

21. Osmer and Douglass, *Cultivating Teen Faith*.

people, adolescents, campus students, and young professionals spanning the ages of fifteen to thirty-five years old in line with the Kenyan definition of youth.[22] These studies combine a creative mix of qualitative and quantitative methods, a diversity of project scopes and sampling methods, as well as broad geographical contexts. Collating her observations of the first four of these, Weber notes the overlapping issues of youth identity and subcultures and how they are shapers of young people.[23] This book will engage with youth subcultures, particularly within the East African context of Nairobi, noting how they function as liturgical actors on young people. Globally, a shallow conceptualization of faith by youth leaders being based on outward behavioral trajectories supports the MTD thesis, which is a failure of youth cultural engagement with the redemptive work of God. Dean further notes that faith formation of young people must be interpreted within a wider sociocultural framework, including the place of parenting and families as well as the historical contexts of young people.[24]

Whereas most of the global studies in youth faith formation are Western, the above studies paint a positive picture with 50 percent of the cited studies located within South Africa. It is necessary to conduct more reflection in the sub-Saharan (SSA) context that is more regionally representative. This is not to mean that there is nothing to learn from the Western context. This means that, for the flourishing of holistic youth ministry, there is need to consider the local contexts and models that will not only be biblically faithful but also relevant to young people in their everyday realities.[25] Thus, a deeper engagement of the faith formation of young people in the African continent is a call to follow Jesus Christ, which is both a call into abundant life (John 10:10) while also being a trans-generational call to young people and children.[26] This call mirrors Jesus' ministry, which is not only personal and privatized (heart, emotions, and will) but public. This can be discerned from Jesus' challenging calls to leaders in the religious, economic, and political spheres.

This book therefore seeks to determine the correlation of these markers with faith formation. Within a global perspective, practitioners and scholars have not always engaged in Christian youth work from

22. Ndereba, "Holistic Approach."
23. Weber, "(South) African Voice," 4.
24. Dean, *Almost Christian*, 3–4.
25. Weber, "Decolonising Youth Ministry Models?"
26. Nel, "Imagine-Making Disciples."

a theological perspective. As a result of this skewed perspective, several theologians have called for a return to theologically driven youth ministry.[27] Practical theologians in the continent have appropriated theological reflection for the African youth ministry context. Aziz has explored issues of youth identity, youth development, and professionalization of youth pastoral work.[28] Chiroma has explored the role of mentoring in youth ministry.[29] Cloete has explored African youth work and faith formation in light of the contemporary digital culture.[30] Much of this research is in the South African context and there is need for a more geographical representation in SSA. By necessity, this will necessitate exploring the concept of identity, particularly in light of the development of theologizing in the continent. This chapter seeks to retrieve the significance of theological identity and its importance for young people in Africa today, much like Kwame Bediako and others such as John Mbiti,[31] J. N. K. Mugambi, Bolaji Idowu, Benezet Bujo did for post-independent Africa within the continent's history of the 1960s–1990s.[32]

PRACTICAL THEOLOGY AS A MEDIATING METHODOLOGY

Although youth ministry is usually located in practical theology, it was not always the case. In fact, Malan Nel places this incorporation of youth ministry in practical theology in the late 1990s and in the early 2000s.[33] The reason given is that since children and youth have for a long time been viewed as part of the family, within the congregational context, youth

---

27. Root and Dean, *Theological Turn*.

28. Aziz, "Youth Identity Discovery"; Aziz et al., "Career Youth Pastor."

29. Chiroma, "Role of Mentoring."

30. Cloete, "Church Is Moving"; Cloete, "Digital Culture"; Cloete, "Youth Culture"; Cloete, "Spiritual Formation."

31. Bediako, *Theology and Identity*; Mbiti, *Concepts of God*.

32. The African theological enterprise has taken several routes on the continent. Scholars have traced themes of decolonization, liberation, and reconstruction within the theologies of key figures such as Allan Boesak, Bolaji Idowu, Benezet Bujo, John Mbiti, Kwame Bediako, and J. N. K. Mugambi. There is also an increasing emphasis on womanist and feminist approaches to theology as examples of contextualized theology in Africa in the work of theologians such as Musa Dube and Mercy Amba Oduyoye.

33. Nel, *Youth Ministry*, 4.

ministry was situated in the discipline of Christian education.[34] Parallel to this, the development of practical theology has been critical in the relationship between youth ministry and theological reflection. Citing this interpretation in the works of the Catholic theologian Thomas Aquinas (1225–1274) and the Lutheran theologian Martin Luther (1483–1546), Malan Nel makes the historical case that theology in the medieval and Reformation eras was not only seen as theoretical but also as practical.[35] Although practical theology during this time was viewed within the scope of pastoral theology, that is the "offices" of the pastor, the turning point is seen through Friedrich Schleiermacher's (1768–1834) widening of the scope from the pastoral office to the congregation.[36] Müller seems to extend Schleiermacher's scope from beyond the congregation to the individual person when he observes that modern practical theology is focused on the values and outlook of a person.[37]

Viewed in this manner, practical theology accommodated the social sciences—for instance in the explication of J. A. Van der Ven,[38] Heitink,[39] and Don Browning[40]—in order to understand human behavior, and it has gone full circle to engage an inter-disciplinary approach. Müller posits that the inter-disciplinary approach has arisen due to the post-foundational epistemological context that undergirds contemporary society, and consequentially, that the cross-pollination of disciplines enriches theological reflection.[41] On the contrary, Klaasen observes the over-reliance on the social sciences when he critiques Browning's approach as one that reduces practice to theory. He offers a more nuanced approach that engages "practical reasoning" throughout the inter-play of theory and practice.[42] However, despite these methodological approaches, practical theologians agree on the role of theology in its engagement with the ordinary issues of life. Wepener, Dreyer, and Meylahn collectively note this outward looking scope of practical theology when they propose that theology must move from individuals to systems and societies

---

34. Nel, "Youth Ministry."
35. Nel, "Youth Ministry," 69–70.
36. Nel, "Youth Ministry," 73.
37. Müller, "Practical Theology."
38. Van der Ven, *Practical Theology*.
39. Heitink, *Practical Theology*.
40. Brown, *Fundamental Practical Theology*.
41. Müller, "Postfoundational Practical Theology."
42. Klaasen, "Practical Theology," 2.

in order to harmonize reconciliation between God, creation, and humanity.[43] Despite its fluidity in engaging across disciplines, practical theology is an ally to the various transformations required in a complex continent.[44]

Thus, practical theology is involved with everyday life. The everyday life of people is raw material for the theologian. In this sense, everyone is a theologian, and everyone engages in theology. Several tools have been offered to help us make sense of God's actions in our everyday life, noting not only the sacred Scriptures or Christian traditions, but also how God shows up in ordinary time. Helen Cameron, Deborah Bharti, Catherine Duce, James Sweeney, and Clare Watkins have developed a tool called the "four theological voices" that can help the practical theologian in analyzing everyday phenomena, which in our case is youth culture among young people.[45] The four theological voices are operant theology, espoused theology, normative theology, and formal theology. Operant theology is the theology that is oftentimes implicit in the lives of people, similar to the computer software that runs in the background of a device. Espoused theology is when this implicit or hidden theology is vocalized. Normative theology refers to what is part of accepted Christian tradition. And formal theology, refers to the careful and systematized understanding usually given by professional clergy or academics. These four ways are helpful as we think about faith formation and how young people have implicit understandings; not only might they vocalize these considering accepted norms but they are also material for the formal systematization for the practical theologian. This is what Ward views as lived theology.[46] Construed this way, the practical theologian has a lot of data to work with in view of the ordinary lives of the youth as well as the actions of God in the larger society.

These "communicative actions" of God in the society are the ripe ingredients for practical theology, a sphere that includes youth ministry based on its unique nature. Nel notes the practices of theological youth ministry as encompassing instruction, preaching, pastoral care, liturgy, fellowship, and administration.[47] What all this means is that youth ministry is not just an exercise in futility, but a divine task full of theological presuppositions and consequences. The tasks of youth ministry such as preaching, teaching, and

---

43. Wepener et al., "Tradition of Practical Theology."
44. Magezi, "Practical Theology in Africa," 135.
45. Ward, *Introducing Practical Theology*, 61.
46. Ward, *Introducing Practical Theology*, 62.
47. Nel, "Youth Ministry," 77.

mentoring and others, are thus necessary for wise theological interpretation in light of the contexts that youth ministry engages on a day-to-day basis. For instance, preaching to young people in a wealthy neighborhood and preaching to young people in a public school near a slum area may be similar and different simultaneously. Within my ministry practice, I have found that working with young people who are fairly privileged calls for emphasis on the gospel around the areas of breaking down societal walls. Engaging young people coming from less-privileged backgrounds means that, while categories of sin are important, it is helpful for them to see how sin structures systems of poverty and cycles of dysfunction, as well as pointing them to the hope and dignity so central to the gospel. Fatherlessness, for example, is an issue that has permeated Kenyan society, yet it is an issue that requires the resources of theological reflection. Elsewhere, I show how Reformed covenant theology can be such a helpful resource in seeking practical interventions, not only in the church but also in the community at large.[48] In this way, while the message of the gospel is beneficial to these varied contexts, it meets unique issues that the youth minister is called to address.

The implications of the preceding exploration of practical theology are of importance to faith formation of youth. Practically, although youth ministry was known to pursue an entertainment focus, youth ministry literature proposed the need to deeply reflect on the practices of young people from a theological angle.[49] This "theological turn" will mean that youth ministry moves from fads to theological reflection in light of cultural location and honoring Christian orthodoxy. This turn would consequentially influence how youth practitioners walk with young people in the sense that practitioners honor the complexity of the lives of young people by becoming God's mouthpiece, hands, and feet in their lives. This would imprint in the youth worker a heart for reaching into the youth's cultural world, understanding its *lingua franca*, and embedding within it the life-birthing, reconciling, sustaining, and completing nature of the gospel of Jesus Christ.[50] And this means that practical theology that leads to this kind of life-renewing gospel work must meet the everyday issues that young people in Africa face, including violence, family trauma, unemployment, postmodern cultural fragmentation, and the struggle for identity.

---

48. Ndereba, "Relevance of Covenant Theology."

49. Dean, *Almost Christian*; Dean, *Practicing Passion*; Strong, "Effective Youth Ministry."

50. Root, *Relational Youth Ministry*; Yaconelli, *Contemplative Youth Ministry*.

DEFINING THE KEY TERMS

Youth

Within the Kenyan context, definitions of young people are based on the Kenya Youth Development Policy (KYDP),[51] the Kenya Constitution,[52] the African Union Youth Charter,[53] and the UN Secretariat. The National Youth Policy (2019) observes that the UN considers "youth" between the age bracket of fifteen to twenty-four years old, the African youth charter between fifteen and thirty-five years, and the Kenya Constitution between fifteen and thirty-four years old.[54] Since this study has the wider African context in mind, it will adopt the African Union Youth Charter's definition of between fifteen and thirty-five years old. Practically, much of youth ministry in Kenya, for instance, is usually geared to this broader age bracket. Further, although youth studies have noted the concept of emerging adulthood as extending the upper limit of adolescence, this book will define adolescence as between thirteen and nineteen years old and young adulthood between twenty and thirty-five years old. Lastly, this book acknowledges the varied definitions of young people in Africa and will therefore use African youth(s) in the plural sense as opposed to in the singular sense, unless the context of usage necessitates it.

Spirituality and Religion

As a precursor to the conversation, it is crucial to differentiate between faith formation and spiritual formation. Defining spirituality is central to understanding the term "spiritual formation." Dallas Willard views spirituality as not only what we do but who we are—as our nature and destiny.[55] He looks at spirituality as that which is non-physical, that is, above the perceptive world. Lastly, Willard looks at the intellectual aspect of spirituality based on the fact that when the spiritual power, person, and self is directed towards a certain subject matter, this falls within the purview of cognition

---

51. State Department for Youth, "Youth Development Policy."
52. Parliament of Kenya, "Kenya Constitution."
53. State Department for Youth, "Youth Development Policy."
54. State Department for Youth, Youth Development Policy."
55. Willard, *Divine Conspiracy*, 79.

or mind.⁵⁶ Thus, Willard envisions spirituality as a matter that touches the whole person, a dimension that stretches beyond time and into eternity.⁵⁷ In the context of youth leaving the church, given the growing realities of "dechurched," "exvangelical," and #MeToo movements, young people continue to debate the place of spirituality and religion. Balswick, King, and Reimer distinguish the two as follows: whereas "religion" has to do with institutional beliefs, "spirituality" is more personal and experiential.⁵⁸ Spirituality in this sense is defined as a "human capacity or quality of a person's character" in which a person has an acute awareness of something greater than themselves.⁵⁹

Combining the concepts of "youth" and "spirituality" has yielded much fruit in contemporary empirical social research.⁶⁰ These scholars observe the historical development of the definition of spirituality from Greco-Roman culture to the enlightenment in order to appreciate its elasticity. They define the term as "a conscious way of life based on a transcendent referent."⁶¹ They list several dimensions arising from their qualitative research with young people—spirituality involves relationship to religion, expression of spirituality, coherence, eclecticism, salience, influence, anthropology, authority, medium, and development. Other scholars note that youth spirituality is linked to the developmental (biological, cognitive, affective) aspects of emerging adulthood—because with increased cognitive capacity, youth are able to reflect on the abstract understandings of God, self, and others.⁶² Other broader factors are influences of socialization—due to the high mobility of young people as a result of employment opportunities and changing social networks—which in turn influence their spirituality. These "socialization factors" that affect youth spirituality include parents, peers, media, and culture.⁶³

---

56. Willard, *Divine Conspiracy*, 80.
57. Willard, *Divine Conspiracy*, 82.
58. Balswick et al., *Reciprocating Self*, 266.
59. Balswick et al., *Reciprocating Self*, 266.
60. Singleton et al., "Spirituality in Adolescence," 247–62.
61. Singleton et al., "Spirituality in Adolescence," 247–62.
62. McNamara et al., "Religiosity and Spirituality," 312.
63. McNamara et al., "Religiosity and Spirituality," 314–17.

Spiritual or Faith Formation

Roberts proposes a symbiotic relationship between spirituality and emotions, when he claims that spiritual maturity is defined through the lens of emotions such as gratitude, hope, peace, and compassion among others.[64] Additionally, he is exclusive in claiming that, beyond a cognitive approach to "belief," Christians must also "attend to the things of God"—this is what Roberts proposes as a basis for spiritual formation.[65] Mulholland defines spiritual formation as "a process of being formed in the image of Christ."[66] In saying this, he differentiates spiritual formation from a self-willed process of control or techniques, with a God-centered process of willful submission to his shaping.

This idea of process is captured by Wilhoit when he defines spiritual formation as nurturing our relationship with God in the company of others for conformity to Christlikeness through the Spirit's working.[67] Within systematic theology in the Reformed tradition, this is akin to the place of sanctification in the Christian life—besides the position of the believer in Christ, sanctification is seen as a life-long process.[68] Some classical practices that enable this formation include prayer, study, fellowship, service, and solitude, which in the Reformed tradition are called the "means of grace."[69] Yet, as James K. A. Smith has observed, these formative practices have been unsuccessful in touching the "desires" of young people in a "consumer-driven" culture that pervades the lives of the young person.[70] These voices affirm the role of the affective aspects of the human person as central for spiritual formation.

In exploring the place of spiritual formation in youth ministry, Chiroma integrates the definitions of other scholars to propose that youth ministry does not exist to solve the problem of youth but to journey with youth as they answer the deep questions about God, faith, identity, purpose, and mission in life.[71] He expands the understanding of faith formation

---

64. Roberts, *Spirituality and Human Emotion*, 12.
65. Roberts, *Spirituality and Human Emotion*, 24.
66. Mulholland, *Invitation to a Journey*, 33.
67. Wilhoit, *Spiritual Formation*, 23.
68. Berkhof, *Systematic Theology*, 534; Calvin, *Institutes*, 258, 378.
69. *Westminster Confession of Faith*, 85, 153.
70. Dean, *Almost Christian*, 5.
71. Chiroma, "Role of Mentoring," 78–81.

to include the process of mentoring young people through narrative sharing, accompaniment, listening, and guiding, for the formation of Christ in young people. Therefore, spiritual formation includes both divine action or will and human responsibility along with intergenerational, trans-cultural, and trinitarian perspectives for the shaping of young people.

Faith Developmental Theory

Faith formation has sometimes been understood as synonymous to or different from the concept of faith development theory. Maddix, Kim, and Riley, for instance, distinguish faith development as a human-based psychological process and faith formation as anchored on a "divine encounter."[72] Fowler, on the basis of this understanding of Piaget and others such as Erikson and Kohlberg, developed the faith development theory.[73] Fowler expanded on the understanding of the cognitive and affective divide by synthesizing "knowing, valuing, and committing" as intertwining aspects of faith. Although Fowler's theory was well received in the 1990s, postmodern sensibilities caused an emergence of other understandings of faith formation.[74] While Fowler based spiritual development on human development, the practical theologian James Loder drew a distinction between the two, suggesting that human development is dependent upon spiritual development and extending the scope of this holistic development to cognitive, moral, and psychosocial spheres.[75] Fowler, for instance, sees faith as a vital and inward process of making meaning of the world.[76] In fact, referencing the Reformed theologians Paul Tillich and Richard Niebuhr, Fowler stretches the scope of faith to a "universal human concern."[77] He goes on to differentiate faith from mere belief or creedal formulations when he notes that faith points to the search of relationship to transcendence.[78] Parrett and Kang understand faith as a meaning-making process, which lies within and outside the confines of organized religion.[79] Thus, faith formation is usually

72. Maddix et al., *Understanding Faith Formation*, 8.
73. Fowler, *Stages of Faith*, 272.
74. Balswick et al., *Reciprocating Self*, 272.
75. Balswick et al., *Reciprocating Self*, 274.
76. Parrett and Kang, *Teaching the Faith*, 224.
77. Fowler, *Stages of Faith*, 5.
78. Fowler, *Stages of Faith*, 14.
79. Parrett and Kang, *Teaching the Faith*, 226.

defined in the light of the different stages of learning that borrow largely from Piaget's theory of cognitive development.

Balswick, King, and Reimer here seem to correlate the concept of faith and spirituality.[80] Others, including Cloete, also view spirituality and faith as synonymous.[81] Setran and Kiesling begin their book on emerging spiritual formation by defining the changing landscape of faith among the next generation in North America and explaining spiritual formation as "a process of reorienting the heart's affections, counting the cost of discipleship, and abiding with Christ in all of life."[82]

In summary, most of the writers have defined spirituality as a holistic concept, one that eschews the predominant dualistic perspective of popular Christianity. These scholars expand faith from a merely cognitive aspect to consider its affective aspect. According to Fowler, some scholars have taken issue with this definition of faith as assumed even in secular contexts.[83] However, this does not affect the place of formation. Formation implies the idea of shaping and processing. Whereas faith formation has generally been thought of in light of human development theory, spiritual formation in Christian literature has more to do with the Christian process of sanctification. Yet we have seen scholars extending the definition of spirituality beyond Christian bounds. In such cases, and for the purposes of this book, the author will use the two terms interchangeably. In other words, "spiritual formation" and "faith formation" are synonymous.

Defined this way, and with the understanding that spiritual formation of young people is crucial to the church, it is possible to proceed forward in different ways. This book will choose to engage the concept of youth culture in general and some sub-cultures in particular. Whether particular ministry emphasis in youth work is teaching or evangelizing or discipling, cultural understanding is necessary in nurturing the faith of young people—as youth workers oftentimes cross cultural boundaries to engage young people according to Walt Mueller.[84] Since the traditional, modern, and postmodern contexts are intertwined in the twenty-first-century African context, how these cultures affect the young person and how the young person affects them is central to our discussion.

80. Balswick et al., *Reciprocating Self*, 275.
81. Cloete, "Spiritual Formation," 70–77.
82. Setran and Kiesling, *Spiritual Formation*, 53.
83. Fowler, *Stages of Faith*, 417.
84. Clark, *Adoptive Youth Ministry*, 118.

Culture

The anthropologist Charles Kraft defines culture as a people's way of life involving their customary ways of living and the implicit worldview assumptions.[85] If the gospel message is to not only take root but also flourish in any cultural context it finds itself in, it must engage it. Richard Niebuhr has offered various typologies of the interaction between gospel and culture that are helpful.[86] The necessity of developing these various models of engagement is premised on the fact that Christian conversion and growth never happen in a nebulous fashion but within concrete and lived realities of people. Therefore, faith formation of African youth cannot ignore youth culture but must consistently engage it. Youth culture may be understood within the broader framework of culture, although it certainly has its nuances. Kraft goes on to show how surface-level culture interacts with deep-level culture in his classifications of the subsystems of economics, politics, religion, social structure, and material culture.[87] While surface-level culture considers particular behaviors, deep-level culture considers values and worldviews that inform those outer behaviors. Yet even the five spheres of culture-making mentioned by Kraft are interpreted differently by each person in space and time. Each person has their own subjective interpretation of these culture-shapers.[88] This consideration of the cultural location of the young person must be an assumption if we are to engage the young person successfully. Young people are oftentimes seen as "suspect youth" as a result of political ideologies, economic constraints, as well as social marginalization in a hierarchical African culture.[89] This understanding of surface-level and deep-level cultures, oftentimes truncated from the contextual location of the young person, is the same understanding that influences how churches develop their implicit or explicit philosophies of youth ministry. In other words, the formation of people is significantly tied to their outer world, and in order to engage them it is necessary to consider these influencers. The following chapter builds upon this chapter by applying theological reflection on an undeniable facet of African societies

---

85. Kraft, *Issues in Contextualization*, 14.

86. Niebuhr, *Christ and Culture*. The New Testament scholar D. A. Carson has offered an evangelical critique of this important work in his book *Christ and Culture Revisited*.

87. Kraft, *Issues in Contextualization*, 18.

88. Root, *Relational Youth Ministry*, 154.

89. Knoetze, "Marginalized Millennials"; Giroux, *Suspect Society*; Nel, "Social Media."

in which young people negotiate—the concept of *ubuntu*, or African communality. The chapter will show that youth ministry after the pandemic can make use of this African heritage, which also mimics what we see as the biblical pattern in the Old and New Testaments.

3

Honoring the Community

FAITH IS A MULTI-LAYERED fabric within the African continent. Envisioned as an awareness of the divine, faith in Africa has been nurtured within a pluralistic religious landscape. To understand these various colors that cast a mosaic of faith, one has to only listen to the songs, the proverbs, the poems—in other words, the oral wisdom—of African peoples. Orobator, the Roman Catholic theologian, extrapolates his faith journey as a multi-phased experience of transitioning from African traditional religion (animism) to Christian faith and practice.[1] He notes how these complex transitions are a commonality of people of faith on the continent of Africa when he borrows the words of the Senegalese poet David Mandessi Diop (1927–1960) in his quintessential "Africa My Africa."[2]

One gleans the often complex histories, geographies, and cultural realities that are present in Africa and that forge the faith of a people. These varied contestations, Orobator argues, dissuade one from an oversimplistic reading of the continent to a more nuanced reading and interpretation of both the continent and her faiths.[3] Through his anecdotal experiences, he writes of his father's animistic experiences and how, in his Christian pilgrimage, he has had to learn to read this way of viewing Africans, using

---

1. Orobator, *Religion and Faith*, 1.
2. Orobator, *Religion and Faith*, 5.
3. Orobator, *Religion and Faith*, 7.

the words of Mbiti, as "incurable believers."[4] While these remain critical intellectual issues to navigate, the role of communities is so central to an African understanding of forming the faith of people, and hence of young people. Since faith is a mediator of divine life and well-being, the role of the communal linkages in African societies are central in understanding how faith develops holistically. Magesa, for example, observes that in ancestral communities, the marital ecosystem and kinship ties are at the core of African societies and have the effect of facilitating the transmission of life to the next generations.[5] Such a communal reading of how faith is formed is different from an individualistic conception that truncates holistic development of young people. Within the biblical canon, faith communities, whether within the unit of the family or within the corporate setting of the *ekklesia*, are central to the transmission of the redemptive message of God and its practical ramifications in the restoration of justice, the upholding of righteousness, and in the facilitation of shalom, all of which are central for the well-being of young people. The role of communities must not be neglected as we think of faith formation.

The reality, however, is that African churches have borrowed an individualistic ethos towards the task of faith formation of their young covenant members. In a bid to aimlessly copy the global cultural force of individualism, African communities of faith may short-circuit the environments within which holistic faith formation happens. A recent trend has been the burgeoning of "youth churches" within the African ecclesiological landscape. Within urban contexts, where a number of young people are nurtured within tense familial backgrounds and where there is a crushing capitalism pushing parents to search for the elusive "more money," young people are in many ways navigating life via the discipleship of TikTok and Netflix, YouTubers and peers—mentorship of young people is happening within the emptiness of an isolated life that is gripped by several types of hurt.[6] I think, for example, of the reality of fatherlessness that is rife within urban cities in Africa, where children and youth are familiar with an emotional, psychological, and spiritual sense of abandonment.[7] Theological categories such as covenant are helpful in dealing with practical societal ailments such as fatherlessness—which is not only physical absence, but

---

4. Orobator, *Religion and Faith*, 19.
5. Magesa, *African Religion*, 77, 110.
6. Clark, *Hurt*.
7. Freeks, "Father Absence and Fatherlessness."

takes the shape of psychological, emotional, and spiritual absence.[8] Thus, when churches move towards the direction of beginning these "youth churches" with little adult involvement, they cut off young people from the life-transmitting context of the wider community. A two-fold return to the African wisdom of community as well as the biblical imperative for an intergenerational approach to youth ministry is necessary.

THE FAMILY IN BIBLICAL CANON

The linkage between African wisdom and the Hebraic tradition on communal thinking is present in the pages of Scripture. The idea of family within Jewish culture and religion is that it is a part of wider kinship relationships.[9] Köstenberger and Jones observe that the Hebraic terms that are related to the concept of family include the concepts of "tribe," "people," and "clan."[10] What emerges from the biblical text, is that God's shalom extends to all families of the world through the family of Abraham (Gen 12, 15, 17).

As part of ancient Near Eastern cultures, the constitution of families was ordered in the following way:

- *patrilineal*—tracing its lineage through the father
- *patrilocal*—married women tracing their lineage to the husband's household
- *patriarchal*—the father being in charge of the household[11]

This reading of the Old Testament family ethics reveals the importance of the family unit. Whereas different approaches to masculinity and femininity espouse divergent views—egalitarian or complementarian—both are called to emphasize the value inherent in both genders. Accordingly, mothers also played important functions in the Israelite communities including naming children, managing households, instructing the children, influencing their husbands, and participating in important public roles.[12] This is also the similar case in many African families and societies. Sudarkasa, for example, noting various anthropological studies on womanhood

---

8. Ndereba, "Relevance of Covenant Theology."
9. Kostenberger and Jones, *God, Marriage, and Family*, 85.
10. Kostenberger and Jones, *God, Marriage, and Family*, 86.
11. Kostenberger and Jones, *God, Marriage, and Family*, 86–88.
12. Kostenberger and Jones, *God, Marriage, and Family*, 89.

in traditional African societies, argues that women played key roles within the extended family (wider kinship network), in political roles, as well as in socioeconomic life—for example, in farming, trading, and crafts.[13] The critical role of parenting for the well-being of children and youth is also evident in the Bible. Among the many duties that parents had were training and teaching their children the way of God, which is central to the understanding of biblical parenting from the Old and New Testament.[14]

A brief survey of the biblical perspective reveals the centrality of the home in God's redemptive acts. Begin in the garden of Eden, we learn that part of how human beings image the creator God is through multiplication, not only in genetic terms but emotionally, spiritually, and creatively as well (Gen 1:26–28; 2:15–17). God's relationship with mankind in the Old Testament is described in covenantal terms—first with Adam, in the covenant of works, but also through the covenant of grace—in its various administrations when God makes covenants with Abraham, Moses, David, Israel, and Christ. In these various schematics, God always intends to be a God to these special people and their children after them (Gen 17:1–8). Central to the covenant community is the telling of these narratives of God's redemptive acts to the next generations (Deut 6:1–9; Ps 78:1–4). Where the adult community fails to entrust the covenant narratives to the next generations, there is chaos and confusion in the society (Judg 2:10). Even in the New Testament, the rituals of the communities of faith such as baptism enact God's inclusion of the next generations in his redemption. Thus, a cursory reading of the Bible places young people not only as recipients of God's redemption but as active agents of God's redemption. The Lord Jesus Christ is incarnated through the womb of a teenage girl, the first elders in the church are young mentees of the apostle Paul (1 Tim 1:1–5; 2 Tim 1:1–5; Titus 1:1–5), and there are both explicit and implicit calls to invest into the next generations in both the home and the church (Eph 6:4; 1 John 2:12–14).

PARENTS AS THE PRIMARY AGENTS OF SPIRITUAL FORMATION

Perhaps the locus classicus of the role of parents in youth spiritual formation is Deut 6:4–25. This passage is founded on the Jewish *shema* that teaches God's nature as one Lord. Parents are commanded to instruct their

---

13. Sudarkasa, "Status of Women."
14. Kostenberger and Jones, *God, Marriage, and Family*, 92–96.

children in the ways of God and to apply their faith to all the facets of their lives—their daily routines, their homes, their fashion, and much more. The chapter shows how parents should seek to respond to the questions that the young people ask—here, by sharing the spiritual significance of Passover as part of God's salvific plan for the covenant people, they are instructed to share their religious tradition and the ethical demand of righteousness.

Two other passages in the Old Testament that negatively affirm the role of adult or parental formation on children is the narrative of Eli's sons in 1 Sam 2:12–26 and the haunting observation in Judg 2:10. Eli's sons display a pattern of carelessness with their priesthood office by participating in sexual immorality and showing negligence of God's Levitical code for the offerings in the temple (1 Sam 2:12, 22; Lev 3:5). Eli then advises them about honoring God through changing their ways, but they remain adamant on their course of action. They are publicly rejected by God. By contrast, the passage records the story of Samuel, the boy who was also ministering in God's house. His mother had been praying for his life purpose, and the priest Eli is able to guide him into his vocation. Similar stories are said of notable Christian saints in the church's history—for example, the role that Monica, Augustine's mother, plays in his own faith formation.[15] Additionally, the Reformed tradition has offered the church a robust foundation for the role of parenting in the covenant nurture of children—that because God makes covenantal relationships with his people and their children, as in the case of Abraham, then parents have both a command and a promise in nurturing their children in the faith.[16] The point is that adults are tasked with significant responsibility in modelling faith and guiding young people into the complexities of the faith journey. The record in Judg 2:10 parallels this: "And all that generation also were gathered to their fathers. And there arose another generation after them who did not know the LORD or the work that he had done for Israel."

Dean has noted that the waning religiosity of teens in American culture is correlated with the lack of robust faith among the parents and older generations.[17] In her incisive chapter on the role of parenting in youth faith formation, she reaches back to Martin Luther and notes that the home is the sanctuary of forming the faith of young people. She goes on to illustrate

---

15. Augustine, *Confessions and Enchiridion*. Haste, "So Many Voices," 6–10; Bouwman, "Spiritual Motherhood," 49–69.

16. Vorster, "Marriage and Family."

17. Dean, *Almost Christian*.

that Luther's *Small Catechism* was primarily designed for use in the home and not in the congregation.[18] The reality that the book of Judges presents is that it isn't that parents will determine the faith development of young people, but that they influence it. This difference is so central in distinguishing between human effort that can burden parents versus faith-fueled parenting of children in the ancient paths.

Wisdom literature is replete with aspects of the role of adults and parents in forming the faith of youth. For instance, Ps 145:4 notes, "One generation shall commend your works to another and shall declare your mighty acts." The context of the passage has to do with the doxology given by all the nations when the Lord accomplishes his redemptive plan to all the world. Part of how this happens is through intergenerational narrative sharing. Older generations are tasked with guiding young people into the path of wisdom, which is personified in and through the person, life, and work of Jesus Christ (1 Cor 1:30). In fact, the book of Ecclesiastes can be pictured as a grandfather's sermons to a younger man after he has experienced the entire gamut of human life—in a sense, it is a theology of existential philosophy that culminates in the foundation of being in a right relationship with God (Eccl 12).

In the New Testament, practical Christian life within the context of the family is predicated upon modelling Christian faith on the side of parents and particularly fathers (Eph 6:4). In the Pastoral Epistles, we find the role of communities in two ways. First, guardians, in the form of parents and grandparents, can significantly contribute to the faith formation of young people (2 Tim 1:5). Paul commends Timothy for his faith, which he later notes was transmitted through his mother Eunice and grandmother Lois nurturing him in the Scriptures "from infancy" (2 Tim 3:14–15). Secondly, we find a model in the pastorals of mature Christians discipling and mentoring younger "proteges." Paul and Timothy are an exemplary model (1 Tim 2:1–2). If Paul is viewed as a youth minister, we can see how complementary youth ministry should be to family discipleship. The point is that adults and parents have a significant role in forming the faith of young people through intentional relationships and processes, within and outside the church.

---

18. Dean, *Almost Christian*, 111.

INTERGENERATIONAL APPROACHES

From this understanding, intergenerational approaches to youth ministry have received considerable attention within contemporary scholarship.[19] Intergenerationality emerged as a focus of youth ministry research and practice as a response towards the age-segregated approach to youth ministry. Proponents of intergenerationally, such as Root and Ward, critique the age-segregation model as a recent innovation in church practice.[20] The intergenerational approach sees the different generations as mutually beneficial to the life of a congregation and seeks to create spaces within the different forms of ministry where this can effectively happen. Thus, an intergenerational approach can be differentiated from the following:

- *Age-separated ministry*—similar to the age-segregated approach, it separates different generational groups based on the perceptions of church leadership on what each group is able to handle.
- *Multi-generational ministry*—the presence of different generations without the full participation or interaction of the groups.
- *Cross-generational ministry*—the presence of different generations, with a unidirectional movement of ministry input from one generation with another.
- *Inclusive ministry*—the inclusion of all generations without any regard for their age.[21]

Nel expands the definition of "inclusive" as rendered by Chancey and Bruner to include the whole congregation in a comprehensive ministry to the youth of the congregation.[22] What Chancey and Bruner observe about the uniqueness of the intergenerational approach is the mutual involvement and reflexivity between the generations. The reason intergenerationality has garnered a lot of support and attention by scholars and practitioners alike is that it speaks to the disconnection that is evident in many congregations that separate the young people from the whole congregation. It becomes more difficult for them to transition effectively into all the aspects of congregational life. Within the Reformed tradition, youth ministry has

---

19. Allen and Lawton, *Intergenerational Christian Formation*.

20. Root, *Faith Formation*; Ward, *Growing Up Evangelical*.

21. Chancey and Bruner, "Guide to Intergenerational Ministry"; Allen, and Lawton, *Intergenerational Christian Formation*.

22. Nel, *Youth Ministry*, 14.

traditionally been practiced within an intergenerational approach. Thus, in the traditional practices of congregations, young people, including children, were present in the worship service from the start to the finish.

Among many Presbyterian congregations in Kenya, this is slowly changing. Several factors influence this. First, there is pressure from mainstream evangelical and charismatic church practice. As churches that have uniquely spearheaded youth ministry practice in contemporary times, what they do is easily mainstreamed within the broader church culture. Second, based on the unique challenge of family dynamics, there are many young people who enter the church as individuals and not in the traditional sense as families. This happens when young people have come from rural places to urban centers to study in the university for example. The new family dynamics also arise from the reality of single-parent families. Usually, when these young people arrive at the church, they naturally build friendships with their peers and fellowships begin. In most cases, youth services have begun from such informal and formal fellowships, especially when critical needs of young people have been met through these ministries.

Although age-separated ministries are a contextual ministry approach, there is need to evaluate how effective they are in the long run. Allen and Lawton unpack the uniqueness of the intergenerational approach as one where different generations can benefit from each other's outlooks, experiences, and ministries.[23] This means that the strengths possessed by each generational group are passed on to the other groups and that the weaknesses are absorbed by the other groups. This is the reason why Aziz observes that the intergenerational approach is critical in the personal development of vulnerable youth as it enables the faith community to build "social capital," which ministers effectively to disadvantaged young people.[24] Some scholars have interpreted such an intergenerational contextualized approach through the "coffee ministry" approach that can be found in some Ethiopian contexts.[25] This approach reconsiders the cultural practice of coffee drinking within Ethiopian culture, and thereby serves young people in light of the socioeconomic, spiritual, and cultural struggles that Africans face and that are not addressed by traditional youth ministry practice in the West.[26] The germaneness of the intergenerational

---

23. Allen and Lawton, *Intergenerational Christian Formation*, 20.
24. Aziz, "Agency of Youth Development."
25. Conner and Molla, "Ethiopian Context."
26. Conner and Molla, "Ethiopian Context."

approach to youth ministry is that it is easily translatable within an African culture where the concept of "community" is present. Whereas modern and postmodern influences are palpable within the African church, the intergenerational approach can be a way of realizing Africa's contribution to the global research and practice of youth ministry.

4

Considering the Power of Music

EVERY MONTH, WE GATHER with some friends to "check the fuel" status of our marriages. These couples have been a wonderful companion for our own marriage, helping us in how we can be intentional in our relationships. In every gathering, we usually have a moment of "checking in" where we share the highlights of the past month. On one occasion, one of the people shared how they happened to have attended a farewell party of a colleague, which happened to have been in an entertainment area—popularly known as a "club." His sharing of the story was to engender some compassion, as he noted that since the day he attended, he can't seem to shake off the songs he heard. He finds himself now bobbing his head and softly singing the lyrics of those beloved, coming of age songs that were once a staple of his "youthful years."

The rise of new media in the past century has been catalytic in cross-cultural flows of ideas and worldviews. In the African context, traditional and postmodern values have ascended to great heights through the wings of digital media. A careful observation of the most watched music videos in Kenya, for example, will reveal this blending of unique African values together with the mishmash of postmodern relativism. The genre of hip-hop music serves as an illustrative example. Ntarangwi informs us that ethnomusicologists have observed a linkage between hip-hop music and African traditional musical expressions. They note some of the hip-hop elements as "call and response, short, repeated phrases and interlocking patterns," which are based on traditional musical expressions such as Nyatiti (eight-string lyre) among the Kenyan and Ugandan musicologists and Dholuo and Obukano (bass lyre) among the Kisii of Kenya.[1] Although hip-hop is a genre that emerged in the context of 1980's New York, it has been localized through the use of local idioms and languages, African spaces and monuments, as well as attired with local dress. Thus, through this cultural expression, the ideals of traditional African values as well as the postmodern ideas of subjectivity and subliminality are embraced and transmitted through music.

A local example is also Sauti Sol, a Kenyan Afro-pop band of international repute. Their lyrics often straddle both cultural forces, even to the extent of exploring theological themes. The lyrics of their song "Kuliko Jana" (translated as "More Than Yesterday") could be seen as a juxtaposition of their song "Short N Sweet." In "Kuliko Jana," the band sings about the steadfast love of God.[2] However, in their other song "Short N Sweet," there is a strong undertone of sexual expression that is common among the liberal values that define much of the Kenyan and global youth culture. A refrain follows that carries sexual undertones, and it is easy to identify the issues of identity, acceptance, culture, love, and religion that are important to the young people.[3] In fact, there was an appeal at the Kenyan Supreme Court in 2019 to change Act 162 of the Constitution, popularized on Twitter as #Repeal162, to encompass more progressive sexual ethics and values.

The African conservative values, for instance, are juxtaposed with the liberal sexual ethos of the West, which stem from the 1960s "sexual revolution" that has now become common place in African villages. Here is a theology of love and on the other hand a liberalization of sexual expression, thereby juxtaposing postmodern ideals with traditional African perspectives. Culture, in this case expressive culture in the form of music, is an important factor for understanding young people so as to minister more effectively to them.

TECHNOLOGY AND YOUTH CULTURE

This hybridity of African traditional values as well as postmodernism in youth culture in Africa has been entrenched by the digital age. Any

1. Ntarangwi, *East African Hip Hop.*
2. Sauti Sol and Aaron Rimbui, "Kuliko Jana."
3. Sauti Sol and Nyashinski, "Short N Sweet."

consideration of youth culture in the globe and in the continent must therefore consider the place of the internet, which, as sociologists observe, largely defines the cultural context of the millennials and Generation Z. One of the most provocative accounts is by Jean Twenge. Twenge looks at how the internet is shaping a more tolerant, less contented, and unprepared generation of young people who find it difficult to transition into adulthood. Her study is based on those born after 1995 (iGens) and founded on four large nationally representative surveys among eleven million Americans since the 1960s. Her earlier doctoral work looked at generational differences between Generation X and millennials and compared them to the differences between the corresponding earlier generations—millennials and iGens; the differences were gradual. What marks iGens is the rapid transformations brought about by the use of the cellphone in the early 2010s, which have transformed their understanding of the world.

Pertinent to the discussion on sexual ethics as a postmodern phenomenon is the reality of social media applications such as Tinder that have increased hook-up culture, advanced multiple sexual partners, led to earlier ages of sexual expression, and delayed long-term relational commitment. For instance, in a comparison with their millennial counterparts, approval of premarital sex increased—from 50 percent of eighteen to twenty-nine-year-olds of the millennial generation to 65 percent of the same demographic of the iGens.[4] On the issue of racial diversity, because iGens are more multicultural in their physical and digital spaces, they are much more inclusive in the area of race. We could stretch this inclusivity to tribes and ethnicity in Africa, although political influence disfigures that cross-cultural salience among young people. Other studies expand the correlation between the internet and sexual ethics, to citizenship, cultural identity, popular music expression, political activism, and agency. In fact, more positively, the internet makes it possible for young people to borrow from foreign cultures and explore positive themes such as the common mantra among millennials, "life, love, and peace," or in the way that hip-hop culture has been acculturated into Chinese youth culture.

In summary, the place of youth culture in faith formation should consider the influence of technology among African adolescents in the twenty-first century. The internet influences youth worldviews and expressions through music, sexuality, identity, political engagement, and spirituality. Since these issues of identity and religion are facets of digital culture as

---

4. Twenge, *iGen*.

well as faith formation, there is need for theological reflection on the same as Cloete has modelled. Thus, faith formation of young people in Africa must include the digital context of the young person and how it influences their way of life. We have also observed that the internet is a feature in the confluence of Western postmodernity and African traditional values, and how these are key in the practical theological reflection of youth ministry.

YOUTH AND CONTEMPORARY CHRISTIAN MUSIC (CCM)

The linkages between Contemporary Christian Music (CCM) and youth cultural expressions have also been explored in various literature. The relationship between the two reveals not only the role that youth culture plays in the faith formation of young people but also how youth culture shapes popular Christian understanding and expression. CCM may be defined as popular music that merges Christian lyrics with contemporary genres and styles of music. These contemporary music genres include pop, rock, hip-hop, and heavy metal, just to name a few. Cusic locates the history of CCM to the counter-culture movements in North American Christianity in the late 1960s and 1970s and sees its growth spearheaded through the booming business of the music industry.[5] Needless to say, as a child of the American evangelical subculture, it has received global impetus through the support of churches and para-church organizations including youth organizations, publishers, and the entertainment industries.

As a musical expression, CCM was an appropriation of the faith into genres that were part of the popular culture. Howard and Streck observe the global discourses and contentions surrounding CCM. First, there is the idea of what constitutes artistic expression that is Christian. Some have critiqued the style of dress, the mode of worship, and the use of, say, tattoos among Christian musicians. According to the critiques, the underlying argument is the relationship between Christianity and culture whereby, according to one of Niebuhr's Christianity and culture models, the two are seen to be antagonistic towards one another.[6] The second critique stems from the interaction between cross-cultural missions and biblical discipleship. Although CCM is premised on the idea of using contemporary forms of music to reach a post-Christian world, some have contended that CCM does little in grounding new Christians into biblical discipleship. CCM has been seen by critics to

---

5. Cusic, *Contemporary Christian Music*.
6. Niebuhr, *Christ and Culture*.

be selective in exploring the doctrines of Christianity that are countercultural while at the same time being a means through which young people are indoctrinated with prosperity gospel and word of faith, which some see as antithetical to the Christian message. For example, Milemba has explored the impact of prosperity theology among youth in contemporary churches whose style of worship is based on the CCM model.[7]

However, some people have interpreted CCM as a genuine mode of Christian worship. Several scholars in the Global South note how the effects of CCM on youth may be negative. Yoon, examining Korean youth, observes that CCM in its highly emotive expressivity hinders a sober reflection between the worshiper and the worshiped (God), is inundated by an extreme individualism, and further entrenches capitalistic ethos whereby CCM is usually a staple for urban and highly mobile congregations.[8] In such congregations, the target is usually the urban young people and families, thereby cutting of those from different socioeconomic classes. Lindhardt explores how Pentecostal Chileans have appropriated youth culture to challenge traditional church structures and create a new identity that interacts with their popular culture.[9] Although Lindhardt commends this as a remarkable feature of innovation and adaptation, the church leaders within those circles are cautious concerning popular cultural influence on their faith. Young also explores the positive effect that evangelical youth culture has had.[10] He observes that evangelical youth culture, globalized through the rise of digital media and through the musical expression of CCM, has found resonance across ideological, political, and religious differences. CCM bands like Hillsong and Bethel have received popular acclaim across the globe: from Cape Town, South Africa, to Nairobi, Kenya, and from Sao Paolo, Brazil, to Berlin, Germany. The question that still remains is whether the premises of CCM are founded on biblical worship or on shifting contemporary cultural impulses.

Within the Reformed tradition, both Carson and Frame understand worship as the God-centered response by the people of God.[11] By expanding worship from merely the contemporary understanding of musical expression or cultural appropriation, the Bible describes worship as a

---

7. Milemba, "Influence of Prosperity Gospel."
8. Yoon, "Tuning in Sacred."
9. Lindhardt, "'We, the Youth.'"
10. Young, "Evangelical Youth Culture."
11. Carson, *Worship by the Book*; Frame, *Worship in Spirit*.

response of the community of faith to the redemptive acts of God. Bloesch carefully observes that though worship employs a wide range of rituals and expressions, it must never be reduced to those forms. When worship is defined merely as an expression, it loses the doctrinal substance, which is the worship of God "in Spirit and in Truth" (John 4:24). Whereas it is appropriate to practice worship in terms that are culturally appropriate to the people, worship is in its essence trans-cultural. This moves beyond the over-emphasis on emotionalism, individualism, and performance, which underpin much of CCM. Secondly, worship within the Reformed tradition is not only what happens during the "singing of hymns" or during "praise and worship," but it is the corporate responses of God's people from the beginning of the Lord's service to the end. According to the earliest Reformers such as Martin Bucer (1491–1551) and John Oecolampadius (1482–1531), these include prayer, singing, preaching of the word, and administering of the sacraments.

By beginning with worship from the biblical standpoint, it can thus be appropriated into a wide variety of cultures while maintaining its core emphasis as a God-centered response of God's people. The Reformed tradition has defined worship through the regulative principle of worship. The narrow definition of this means that the Bible should strictly define how we worship, and those who interpret it this way only permit exclusive psalmody and/or hymnody in congregational worship. Those who define it in a broader sense make room for wider expressions, styles, and forms of music, with the condition that the lyrics are doctrinally sound. What this section shows us is how much sensitivity and wisdom is needed in exploring the place of youth culture in Christian culture. Contextualizing the forms of Christian expression such as worship in order to engage youth popular culture must be done in a manner that is thoughtful, relevant, and ultimately biblical.

5

Navigating iGens and Digital Church[1]

IN MANY WAYS, THE COVID pandemic has transformed the world. From its genesis as a novel virus, it has emerged as a landmark second pandemic after the Spanish flu of 1918. With its beginnings in Wuhan, China, the severe, acute respiratory syndrome, coronavirus 2 (SARS-CoV-2), has touched every corner of the globe.[2] Several years into the virus, many people have given due attention to the effect of the virus on issues as disparate as mental health, business start-ups, educational systems, and religious organizations. Within the Kenyan context, scholars at Daystar University have addressed what the post-COVID church context would look like given the ongoing pandemic and its ramifications on the public health and technological landscape.[3] These multi-disciplinary perspectives unpack the role of the church in dealing with the sociological, developmental, and educational issues in light of the COVID pandemic. In this chapter, I focus the conversation on the interface between the church and the swelling reality of the digital context that she finds herself in, within the post-COVID pandemic.

Interestingly, 2021 emerged as the year where significant technological changes have touched the world. Conversations on cryptocurrencies,

---

1. Chapter 5 is derived with permission from my 2022 Acta Theologica article: Ndereba, "Relevance of Covenant Theology."

2. Liu et al., "COVID-19."

3. Munyao et al., *African Church and COVID-19*.

transhumanism, Artificial Intelligence (AI), and Augmented Reality (AR) are part of the global conversation on what life within the "metaverse" will actually look like.[4] Jun explores church planting for Virtual Reality (VR) and how this creates both opportunities and challenges.[5] By and large, he grounds his reflections on Han Küng's ecclesiology, which holds in tension the concept of church as form and church as essence.[6] Rather than taking an isolationist perspective, he observes that "if masons, architects, and artists were needed to build physical spaces for worship in the past, we need coders and futurists to build this unprecedented style of church in the metaverse."[7] The implications for Christian life—what grounds human meaning and purpose—are gaining traction in the conversation. What do these digital transformations mean for Christian life and the concept of being church? These broader conversations are the ever-widening boundaries for the discussion of church and the digital space. COVID-19 has functioned as a sort of accelerator for these conversations in wider culture. For the innovators and early adopters, it has created a momentum for widening the scope of ministry, while the late adopters of these technological changes have prolonged their responses on what these dynamic changes portend for the church.

While several churches, particularly within urban contexts, have integrated digital media as part of their ministries, some churches and church leaders have been antagonistic towards the place of technology in the church's spiritual mission. Nonetheless, with the closing of churches in Kenya on March 13, 2020 through the multi-phased approach, digital integration moved beyond a proposal to the only way of maintaining continuity in the church's ministry. In Kenya, a survey was conducted between May 22 and June 20, 2020 by ShahidiHub Africa to explore the church's response to the pandemic. The open survey examined 429 leaders, thirty-three counties, and 161 denominations in Kenya. Two major pastoral responses were opening new social media accounts or reactivating social media platforms that were dormant in the past.[8] A follow-up survey in 2021, after churches had been reopened, revealed that a considerable number of churches continued with a hybrid version of ministry, with 57.59 percent of leaders

---

4. Anderson, *Technology and Theology*.
5. Jun, "Virtual Reality Church."
6. Jun, "Virtual Reality Church," 1.
7. Jun, "Virtual Reality Church," 7.
8. ShahidiHub Africa, "Research Poll Release," 2020.

offering both online and in-person services.[9] Although the online mode of ministry experienced some challenges, various strategies were offered to deal with the challenges. These sentiments are shared across other regions of the world and reveal the church's adaptability within the wake of the COVID pandemic along with its interaction with constitutional law and state mandates.[10] What is evident is that digital technology is an important factor in the church's ministry and mission. An interesting role has been the place of "digital natives," or young people who have been critical voices in the church's transition towards online ministry in the post-COVID dynamic.[11] The reality of ministry after the pandemic is that younger and older generations must work together in order to enflesh God's mission to the whole world. While young people have helped the church to deal with the digital transformation, they have also been largely affected in the area of mental well-being. The need for all generations to share the ministry of Jesus Christ to one another remains.

APPROACHING THE ONLINE CHURCH CONVERSATION

While this book offers a practical theology from the Global South, this chapter applies that framework to the emerging field of digital ecclesiology. Whereas ecclesiology is a discipline of systematic theology, the role of digital technology in the transformation of the church's life and practice necessitates a mode of reflection that is suited to the strength of practical theology. Practical theology helps us to make use of vast knowledge domains and how they intersect with particular theological ideas and practices. In this season, churches have grappled with the practice of holy communion (or the Lord's Supper), the challenges of fostering belonging through online fellowships, as well as the missional challenge of reaching out to a generation that is more disillusioned with church attendance. This chapter furthers the conversation by borrowing from a Reformed understanding of church in conversation with some of the ideas that have emerged from what is called digital ecclesiology.

I engage this chapter by asking four sets of questions that have been proposed by a well-known practical theologian, Richard Osmer. These

---

9. ShahidiHub Africa, "Research Poll Release," 2021.
10. Asamoah-Gyadu et al., "Pandemic and World Christianity."
11. Cloete, "Church Is Moving," 27–31.

questions can help us to get underneath the challenges and prospects of the digital mode of ministry after the pandemic.

1. The descriptive question—What is happening within the digital cultures that the next generations are immersed in?
2. The interpretive question—Why is this happening?
3. The normative question—What models of church do we have from either the biblical precedence or theological tradition, or in this case, Reformed ecclesiology?
4. The pragmatic question—How does this inform the prospects and challenges of doing church among digitally native Africans?[12]

To answer the first question, I will show how understanding the transformations of the iGens can help us to understand how digital media has shaped rising generations. The challenge is usually to assume that young people are all the same. But understanding the culture that they belong to can enable us to make some inroads in terms of meaningful ministry among, with, and to them. The second question seeks to answer the question on the challenges arising with ministry to young people within the digital context. I think that listening to some of the ideas and issues that have arisen from the whole conversation of "online church" may serve our purpose well. The third question explores the theological resources that we can explore as a way of answering what should be happening. Making use of my own Christian heritage, I engage with the theology of church found in the work of Louis Berkhof (1873–1957), a theologian in the Reformed tradition. His insights of church as organism and as an institution can help us to enter more fully into the missional opportunity rather than lamenting how much young people have not returned to church—and usually, when we say this, we mean the traditional and institutional way of doing things. Reminding ourselves that the church is an organism can help us to deal with notions of church that arise from a perspective of power rather from a posture of prayer and mission. Lastly, we will think about the challenges and prospects that this has for engaging young people within the digital world.

---

12. Osmer, *Practical Theology*, 4.

DIGITAL ECCLESIOLOGY AND AFRICA'S iGENS

The interaction of the church and digital space has received recent attention in the last ten years within the field of digital ecclesiology. This budding field of interdisciplinary reflection has usually taken two varied approaches.[13] The first approach explores the usefulness of digital modes of communication and tools within the practical ministry of the church. The second approach explores the impact, either positive or negative, on the church's role and mission. This chapter delves into this contemporary discussion that has been necessitated through the digital context of a post-COVID world.

The digital landscape has affected five major themes surrounding the religious life of churches.[14] These are ritual, identity, community, authority, and authenticity. Rituals within different religions function as physical actions that mediate the divine. The domain of ritual studies has engaged a multiplicity of views, but some see rituals as either structured and formal or spontaneous and personally constructed.[15] Within Christian theology, sacraments are forms of rituals in a broader sense. The COVID-19 pandemic has generated significant debate surrounding the validity of taking communion online. Some questions include: Is the practice of online communion valid? Also, Do the members of the church have to be physically present in order to participate in sacramental practices? The digital space has forced congregations to wrestle with such questions. Whereas churches may have written down liturgies and even theologies of how they understand sacraments or how sacraments should be practiced, the uniqueness of the COVID-19 pandemic raised new questions for normative practices of congregations.

Lovheim explores how the rise of social networks in the 2000s changed how people interact with media, moving from mere consumers to producers of content.[16] In our 2025 context, young people no longer have to traverse the traditional initiatory rites in their journey towards adulthood, but on the click of a button they can develop content that significantly shapes the opinion of their followers. This emerging reality of the agency that the technological world presents for young people raises certain issues such as privacy, virtual reality, as well as early success, which significantly shape

---

13. Campbell, *Digital Ecclesiology*.
14. Campbell, *Digital Religion*.
15. Campbell, *Digital Religion*, 27.
16. Campbell, *Digital Religion*, 44.

the identity of digital natives today. The digital world of the young person today also influences the idea of authority, because currently, young people can listen to a physical preacher on a Sunday service while checking out the sermon outline of a famous online preacher in another part of the world. I have had instances where, in my conversation with young people, someone remarked, "Yes, it reminds me of what Pastor Michael Todd was saying about relationships the other day."[17] All these factors are paramount for the church in the post-COVID context.

The emerging research in this budding field is clearly correlative of the context of the digital natives in the world at large. Digital natives have been referred to as *iGens* (those who have grown up in the wake of Steve Jobs's iPhone) and span three broad generational bands: millennial, Generation Z (Gen Zs), and Generation Alpha (Gen As).[18] Millennial (born between 1981 and 1996), Gen Z (born between 1997 and 2012), and Gen A (born between the early 2010s and mid-2020s) are three broad ways of construing the sociological markers of young people within generational thinking. As of 2025, the oldest millennial is forty-four and the youngest Gen Z is ten years old. While Gen A is an evolving concept, what these three groups share is their digital adaptability, with the younger ages even more exposed to various digital platforms at a younger age and with more complexity.

In terms of the sociocultural and economic issues, millennials in Kenya were part of the nation during its transition from a single-party state to a multi-party state, experienced the effects of the Structural Adjustment Programmes (SAPs), and together with the Gen Zs, experienced the explosion of the internet—with the onset of emails in the 1980s, the World Wide Web in the early 1990s, and social media networks and blogs such as LinkedIn and Facebook in the early 2000s.[19]

Gen Zs and Gen As are more familiar with video games and Virtual Reality as well as a variety of consequential ethical issues that arise from being immersed in this new world. Some of these issues include cyberbullying, pornography, anonymity, and media manipulation.[20] Additionally, the digital reality further complicates the question of identity, with social

---

17. Michael Todd is a famous African American preacher who has a wide following on digital platforms. He is known for his contemporary preaching that speaks to the issues of young people.
18. Twenge, *iGen*.
19. Palfrey and Gasser, *Born Digital*.
20. Ess, *Digital Media Ethics*.

media offering varied ways of self-representation for teenagers who may grapple with their self-image in a way that is uncommon for the "analogue age."[21] What does this mean for Christian congregations? First, pastoral care must be directed towards emerging issues such as fragmented identities. In a world where young people living in between two worlds, it is difficult for them to distinguish between the real and the illusory. Second, the digital world presents an interesting challenge for discipleship. Young people are influenced by so many voices meaning that nurturing Christian fellowship in an age of anonymity and constant connectivity requires much more from those who disciple young people. Third, preaching as the authoritative proclamation of the gospel to the contextual issues that people face is challenged by the power that is vested among digital influencers, thereby changing how young people view churches as institutions of "religious power." In my view, this last challenge may be helpful for us to rediscover the church as an organism, which is a concept that emerged very strongly from the early church in the New Testament.

However, this does not mean that we view technology as an evil brought to us from the abyss of hell. Within the African context, some church leaders always demonized technology based on their consideration of the challenges that it raises for contemporary life. Moving beyond these challenges, I want to reshape an overly antagonistic stance to digital media, noting how technology has created a boon for the church. Let me offer you a few examples. You are enjoying reading this book, hopefully, because you can actually read it, right? This printed book (or its online version) is made available by technology. In fact, the printing press was catalytic for growth of the Protestant Reformation, which some of us derive our spiritual heritage. In contemporary practice, technology has helped us to grow in our Christian life because we now have access to the messages, sermons, and writings of Christian leaders through the internet and other social media. The role of technology in the life of the church can be seen through the print culture that produced hymnals and biblical translations, to the role of radio and television in 1930s evangelism and 1960s televangelism.[22] As a part of youth culture, the narrative of media merits a deeper reflection rather than a simplistic rejection as young people utilize media for positive uses, including good entertainment, educational progress, and spiritual growth.

---

21. Palfrey and Gasser, *Born Digital*, 22.
22. Asamoah-Gyadu et al., "Pandemic and World Christianity," 217.

Aspects of Reformed Ecclesiology

What is clear is that the global digital transformation is an ongoing process that requires much more consideration. Whereas digital ecclesiology focuses on the practical side of ecclesiology, theological reflection on the nature of the church and its mission is equally useful. I think that one of the benefits of appreciating the history of the global church is that we appreciate that the Holy Spirit has been at work in the church throughout the ages. It should never be the case that we view our current generation as the generation that has it all figured out. It is true that there are also "ghosts from the past" that haunt the church, but it is also helpful to consider the good from history. In my own view, I think that the Reformed understanding of the church can give us some bearing as we seek to navigate the contemporary context of the digital world. More specifically, the insights that we can draw from Louis Berkhof's understanding of the church as well as one of the classical Christian confessions, the *Westminster Confession of Faith* (*WCF*), can help us to grapple with the biblical perspective on the nature and role of the church, as has been mediated through the Reformed tradition. This theological reflection seeks to engage a particular context (digital culture), while reading the Bible through a particular theological tradition (theological context). This undergirds the point that there is no *tabula rasa* in theological reflection. By owning up to one's tradition, one is better able to address both the strengths and weaknesses that may arise in this mediation of cultural context and biblical-theological content.

The Nature of the Church

Louis Berkhof is chosen as a theologian due to his enduring influence on Reformed theology. In terms of his influence, his *Systematic Theology* ranks as second only to Calvin's *Institutes of Christian Religion* as a formative systematic treatment of Christian doctrine in the reformed tradition. He was born in Emmen, in the Netherlands, and together with his family moved to Grand Rapids, Michigan in 1882. He was a graduate of Calvin Theological Seminary in 1900, and pastored Michigan First Christian Reformed Church in Allendale. He received a BD degree from Princeton in 1902 and then pastored the Oakdale Park Church in Grand Rapids. He joined the faculty of Calvin Theological Seminary in 1906, becoming its president in 1931, and serving until 1944. Berkhof married Reka Dijkhuis in 1928, and their marriage was blessed with four children: Grace Meyer, William, Jean Stuk, and John. Later, in 1984, he married Dena Heyns-Joldersma who had two daughters: Joanne Heyns De Jong and Wilma Heyns Brouwer.[23]

Berkhof's chapter on the church closely follows his chapter on the application and work of redemption. This is interesting because it reveals that to him, the church finds its source in the redemptive work of God in Christ. As a contrast, the Roman Catholic position is that the understanding of God is anchored on the doctrine of the church. Consequently, Berkhof's view is that the church is not only or primarily an institution, but a "spiritual organism."[24] Berkhof connects the doctrine of the church to the doctrine of Christ when he categorically states that "there is no church apart from the redemptive work of Christ and from the renewing operations of the Holy Spirit."[25] We see this "organism" of the church, meaning that in a very elementary way the church is a bearer of new life. Even if young people are disinterested with the church as an institution, it doesn't mean that they are disinterested with church as an organism. In fact, I think what the digital moment offers the church today is to recover this organism of the church.

To further explore the nature of the church, Reformed theologians have distinguished between the visible and invisible aspects of the church.[26] The invisible church is made up of all believers of Jesus Christ in space and time. Visible believers gather together in local churches that are distinct in geography, space, and time. Thus, this makes room for conceiving of those who belong in the invisible and visible aspects of the church, while also making room for a dynamic understanding of the church's mission. Berkhof puts it this way: "The church forms a spiritual unity of which Christ is the divine Head . . . and is destined to reflect the glory of God as manifested in the work of redemption."[27] This means that the church is always accessible to all people, without regard to physical buildings and meetings that were largely curtailed during the pandemic. It is true that there is a special connection that comes from physical gathering, but there is always a possibility of gathering with the "invisible church" when physical gathering is unavailable. One of the greatest things I witnessed during the pandemic was a renewed unity between Christians across the globe. I

---

23. Calvin Theological Seminary, "Presidents of Calvin."
24. Berkhof, *Systematic Theology*, 12.
25. Berkhof, *Systematic Theology*, 553.
26. WCF 25:1.
27. Berkhof, *Systematic Theology*, 565.

have participated in many more global gatherings of Christians than in the past because in a new sense we in the Global South appreciated how united we were in light of the global foe of the virus as well as the singular mission of Jesus Christ that binds us together.

Clearly, there is a distinction between the church as organism, *apparitio*, and the church as institution, *institutio*.[28] Berkhoff compares the concept of organism and institution when he notes that, as an organism, the church is described as communion through the bonds of the Holy Spirit, whereas as institution, the church takes up particular organizational forms with various offices for administrative purposes.[29] Never divorced from each other, the two concepts are mutually beneficent: "The church as an institution or organization is a means to an end, and this is found in the church as an organism, the community of believers."[30] What this means is that church structure (or even doctrine) for that matter is not an end in itself, but it is to serve God's redemptive purposes for his body. This distinction is helpful for us, particularly as we engage young people who have a disdain for structure and who are more dynamic in terms of authority structures. Both wisdom and sensitivity are required, particularly as we consider how digital cultures have created a fluid sense of definition for digital natives. The question remains, how do these distinctives inform our practical mission to digital natives?

The Mission of the Church

Again, borrowing from my own Reformed heritage, the mission of the church is viewed primarily in spiritual terms. So, for instance, Berkhof observes that the church as the kingdom of God takes on an eschatological significance in its mission to establish "the rule of God . . . in the hearts of sinners by the powerful regenerating influence of the Holy Spirit, insuring them of the inestimable blessings of salvation."[31] Likewise, the *Westminster Confession of Faith* (*WCF*) observes,

> Christ has given the ministry, oracles, and ordinances of God, for the gathering and perfecting of the saints, in this life, to the end of

---

28. Berkhof, *Systematic Theology*, 567.
29. Berkhof, *Systematic Theology*, 567.
30. Berkhof, *Systematic Theology*, 567.
31. Berkhof, *Systematic Theology*, 568.

the world: and does, by His own presence and Spirit, according to His promise, make them effectual.[32]

While this "ultimate end" of the mission of the church is laudable, we can say that within Reformed ecclesiology in Africa, Reformed churches have contributed to the well-being of the communities. Whereas some scholars have rejected the relevance of social justice as a critical mission of the church, the context of Africa's economies and societies cannot ignore ministry to "the least of these"—while gospel ministry is primary, so is the pursuit of justice and shalom as part of the church's calling. A number of African theologians in different Christian traditions have explored the relevance of ecclesiology within the African landscape of communalism, healthcare, and other cultural issues. Orobator, for instance, observes that while the origin of the church can be traced to the life of Jesus Christ, the New Testament provides principles of the church but there is need for "creative imagination" in how that should function in the context of community and kinship ideas in African communities.[33] On a similar vein, Nyamiti has also utilized his "ancestor Christology" to conceive of the church as the body that has Christ as the chief ancestor, with believers being descendants of Christ and therefore connecting them to the global church in time.[34] These thinkers try to grapple with the understanding of African realities. As Reformed ecclesiology emerged from within particular medieval excesses of Roman Catholic ecclesiology, ecclesiology in contemporary African context must also engage the realities of the day that arise from digital cultures. Both the former and latter are evidence of the need for contextualization as we think of how Christian doctrine touches the everyday realities in diverse places. Thus, contemporary theological reflection must navigate the discourse between the church's ministry and the implications of digital technologies without carelessly transposing ecclesiology from one context to another.[35] Following the thesis that the COVID-19 pandemic is a "kairos moment," and if as Mwambazambi claims, ecclesiology must follow missiology, then we must consider the implications of digital ecclesiology today.[36] Consequently, with the above reflections, we ask, How can we discern God's mission for the church in this digital post-COVID context and

32. *WCF* 25:3.
33. Orobator, "Perspectives and Trends," 269.
34. Nyamiti, "Christ's Ancestral Mediation," 129–77.
35. Campbell and Dyer, *Digital Church*.
36. Mwambazambi, "Reflection on African Ecclesiology," 1–8.

what does this mean for Africa's next generations? The following section unpacks what this looks like among the lives of young people in Africa.

PROSPECTS AND CHALLENGES

The critical issues raised so far help to orient the discussion of what church looks like and what it is called to do within the context of digital natives. As those whose daily lives are part of digital reality, the church must continuously reflect on its nature and mission to and with them. The conversation around digital ecclesiology explores a wide range of issues, including how digital technology is changing concepts such as identity, authority, and community. On the other hand, we have seen how the nature of the church is timeless, yet its mission must be concrete within the lives of young people. In this section, we explore some prospects and challenges of church in a digital and post-COVID landscape.

Several prospects emerge from this chapter. First, the digital landscape provides an opportunity for the church for missional engagement of unengaged or disengaged youth. While religion plays a critical role in the lives of Africans, and particularly young people, there are pockets of non-religious youth in different parts of the continent. Since these youth may not physically come to the church, the digital space presents an opportunity for the church to go to them. This means that churches must design digital strategies that allow the ministry of the church to reach out to young people in the context of the digital world. Second, digital ecclesiology, particularly within a post-COVID context, expands the church's understanding as an organism vis-à-vis the concept of the church as institution. This chapter revealed that most churches experienced drastic changes in their ministries, particularly with young people. While the dialogue is still an important one, it could be argued that the post-COVID digital context allowed congregants to sample different liturgical orientations, worship spaces, and preaching forms that differ from their own backgrounds. By doing this, the thinking of the church has been expanded to consider the strengths of different denominations in a manner that fosters mutual fellowship and dialogue in a way that was not possible in the past. All these mean that the church has been united in many ways and the digital landscape creates an opportunity for churches to engage in common mission. In many ways, digital ecclesiology presents room for the church's mission in the world.

In terms of challenges, various issues emerge from the context of digital media. First, while the digital landscape expands the idea of community, it also changes what exactly that means. In other words, while people can participate in various networks on the online space, they can do so in an individualistic, isolated, and consumeristic sense that may hinder the ministry of the church. For example, the church is called to participate in deeds of mercy and justice. While the digital space allows for people to contribute to the church's mission through online money platforms, the lack of physical immersion into the actual mercy ministry engagement takes away a particular concreteness that helps them to discern God's call within particular sociocultural contexts. Second, while the digital landscape expands the opportunity for online mentorship and discipleship, people still lose a life-on-life discipleship that fosters deep learning and understanding. For instance, in the Paul–Timothy model, the apostle commends Timothy to follow him based on what he has observed, seen, and heard (1 Tim 2). Since one of the primary ways of learning, particularly in youth ministry contexts, happens through observation, how might we engage this barrier in our youth ministry practice in the digital environment? Lastly, while the digital habitat means that we have an appreciation of the invisible and organic church, what might this mean for the intertwined concepts of membership, church discipline, and sacramentology? As Campbell argues, the technological landscape has transformed place-based community to the concept of "networked individualism" where people derive their social and spiritual capital from their chosen networks rather than from an ecclesiastical institution.[37]

This chapter reveals that the digital landscape presents critical points of interrogation for the nature and mission of the church. The research in digital ecclesiology helps us to consider some of the salient issues. This chapter has proposed that as opposed to an isolationist or assimilationist approach to new media and technology, the church is called to wise and discerning engagement with the digital landscape. These have been listed as prospects and challenges by way of commendation and reflection as we consider how God may still be at work within this "kairos moment." These realities also present unique challenges for pastoral care, especially in light of the emerging issues that the pandemic has brought. To this, we need to also explore the important element of caring for young people in the wake of the pandemic.

---

37. Campbell, *Digital Religion*, 68.

6

Caring for Young People After the Pandemic[1]

PASTORAL CARE IS A foundational element in youth ministry practice, yet one that is often neglected. This neglect arises from the fact that the lives of young people are rich and informed by unique issues. Several challenges in mental health and sexuality issues among young people have emerged after the pandemic. It isn't that they were not there before, but the pandemic brought them to the foreground. These changes were necessitated by the transitions that were affected in the lives of young people, for example their educational progress, their sociopsychological support, as well as their absence of peer networks. In this chapter we hear from youth leaders in the Presbyterian Church of East Africa (PCEA) and how they navigated these issues. We will also learn from the long tradition of pastoral care in the church and how this can inform the caring approach and practices of churches and especially youth ministry.

UNDERSTANDING PASTORAL CARE

Pastoral care, *cura pastoralis*, is a subdiscipline within pastoral theology, or in contemporary usage, practical theology, that has to do with the

---

1. Chapter 6 is derived with permission from Ndereba, "Youth Transitions."

compassionate response by Christian leaders to the people of God under their care. Nel considers it as a mode of ministry connected to other facets such as preaching, administration, and fellowship, but one that remains a neglected yet very crucial in the ministry with and to children and adolescents.[2] When directed towards the young members of the communities of faith, it is a critical reminder to them that God is with them through the entire journey of the human experience. In this light, pastoral care is a critical ministry towards the people of God with various elements central to its task. These include understanding, listening, empathy, presence, and guidance.

In the biblical canon, it is encapsulated in the image of God as shepherd in the Old Testament (Gen 48:24; Ps 23; Isa 53; Jer 49:19; 50:44). In the New Testament, pastoral care is incarnated among God's people through the residence of God himself in the person and work of Jesus Christ who is called the chief shepherd (Heb 13:20; 1 Pet 5:4). In his ascension, this mode of ministry of *cura pastoralis* is continued by those members of the communities of faith uniquely called to shepherd God's people (Acts 20:17–38; Titus 1–2; 1 Pet 5:1–4). However, within the New Testament practice, it is clear that pastoral care can also be exercised by ordinary members and not just those in official positions of leadership in the church (Rom 14:17–19; 1 Cor 12:4–7; 1 Thess 5:11). In fact, those who see youth ministry as a function of the entire congregation argue that pastoral care is the responsibility of the whole church to all her members. Pastoral care has also been connected to the gospel, especially to how God's actions of reconciling, leading, healing, encouraging, and renewing are ways of making the gospel real and tangible to people.[3]

Pastoral care is not new in the church. By looking at some of the church's formative pastors and theologians, Purves has provided a historical treatment of pastoral theology. He does this by analyzing the reflections and pastoral work of pastoral theologians such as Gregory Nazianzus (329–390), John Chrysostom (347–407), Gregory the Great (540–604), Martin Bucer (1491–1551), and Richard Baxter (1615–1691).[4] Within the Reformed tradition, pastoral care is not a separate work from the word and sacraments as means of grace but an extension of the same. As an expression of practical theology, it is grounded in the classical disciplines of historical and systematic theology. Historical theology studies the development of dogmatics in

---

2. Nel, *Youth Ministry*, 235.
3. Nel, *Youth Ministry*, 227.
4. Purves, *Pastoral Theology*.

the different church eras such as the apostolic era, the early church era, the medieval era, Reformation era, post-Reformation, and modern eras. Systematic theology on the other hand expounds on key doctrines of the Christian faith. Practical theology utilizes historical and systematic theology by applying their insights to specific issues and within particular contexts, noting how they inform practices and are reformed by them. Thus, pastoral care connects the power of the gospel to the actual lives of people.

Pastoral care has emerged as a distinctive aspect of pastoral work and theological reflection in the last century. Lartey explores the various definitions of pastoral care explored by different scholars and notes five different aspects of pastoral care:

1. An expression of human concern
2. Acknowledgement of the transcendent aspect of life
3. Utilization of viable communication methods between pastoral care giver and the one cared for
4. The motive of love
5. The dual aims of either prevention of harm or fostering of an abundant life[5]

What Lartey offers in the conventional understanding of pastoral care is the influence of cultures in mediating thinking and practice, and consequentially, an inter-cultural approach to pastoral care that provides a more holistic and dynamic perspective.[6] Therefore, pastoral care may be seen as a critical nurturing activity of the church towards her members for their holistic well-being. Within the *ekklesia*, this may be conducted by pastors or official church leaders, but similarly, by the ordinary church member. This is why some have engaged the study of pastoral care within the context of education institutions and consider the pastoral care function played by teachers or other appropriate personnel.[7] In recent global scholarship, pastoral care has been approached from ethnographic methods, from postcolonial hermeneutic methods, advances in neuroscience, as well as the intersections of race, religion, and gender in light of socioeconomic and sociocultural transitions in various societies.[8]

---

5. Lartey, *In Living Color*, 25–30.
6. Lartey, *In Living Color*, 36.
7. Collins and McNiff, *Rethinking Pastoral Care*.
8. Ramsay, *Pastoral Theology and Care*, 1.

Models and Methods in Pastoral Care

Lartey envisages pastoral care in five models.[9] He views pastoral care as therapy, ministry, social action, empowerment, and personal interaction. These models of pastoral care also result in various methods in pastoral care. If the models can be understood as the overall framework, methods are how the framework is actualized within real pastoral contexts. Within the wake of the COVID-19 pandemic, church responses have coalesced around these models. For instance, in a survey that was conducted between May 22 and June 20, 2020 by ShahidiHub Africa to explore the Kenyan church's response to the pandemic, several issues emerged.[10] The open survey examined 429 leaders, 33 counties, and 161 denominations in Kenya. From the study, pastors have gently walked with grieving families to offer them comfort and consolation; local congregations have been at the forefront of offering food and shelter to those with acute basic needs when people were laid off from work; and youth pastors have been at the center of youth empowerment when invitations arose from public schools facing mental health issues among their young people. This chapter will reveal how this actually happened and how this informs pastoral care practice in African youth ministry.

One of the popular methods in pastoral care and practice is the narrative approach. Wimberly, for instance, lists storytelling and story-listening as transformative practices in African American communities.[11] This approach combines the mutual experiences of the pastoral care giver, the intimacy of caring relationships, God's unfolding story of redemption, and the exploration of possible solutions to the specific problems. Dreyer also applies the narrative approach through the coping life story of a young adult, thirty-three-year-old *Idols* contestant Lloyd Cele, to the emerging adulthood issues that include identity, discovery, peer pressure, career selection, poverty, and politics.[12] These issues are salient feature of the lives of African youth. Given these lived realities, Dreyer sees the aim of pastoral care as expanding the imagination of young people beyond their immediate limitations.[13] Central to the aim of pastoral care giving is to point young people

---

9. Lartey, *In Living Color*, 55–59.
10. ShahidiHub Africa, "Research Poll Release," 2020.
11. Wimberly, *African American Pastoral Care*.
12. Dreyer, "Reframing Youth."
13. Dreyer, "Reframing Youth," 2.

to the transcendent God. This also fits in with Patton's paradigm of pastoral care as a practice of rehabilitating God's relationship with people within a community of human relationships. Christian pastoral care is therefore theological in nature.[14]

Pastoral Care Issues facing Young People

Pastoral care in the context of the local congregation has to do with the care and cure of souls by the pastoral leadership for people's personal and vocational transformation in light of God's redemptive story.[15] Fowler situates it in the field of practical theology, which seeks to dissolve the barriers between "hard theology" and "soft theology." Pastoral care may therefore be exercised more specifically among young people. The two primary places that young people may be found are the church and educational institutions. Pastoral care in the educational context of young people has been well researched and documented. Since work with young people typically happens within educational institutions, pastoral care and counseling is practiced by trained teachers or chaplains who serve that critical function. Thus, it has been seen as a teacher's role in the guidance and counseling process of young people in school.[16] In the local church, pastoral care may be exercised by the senior pastor, the elders, deacons, youth leaders, or other adults. As such, it may take the form of guidance and counseling, mentoring, peer-to-peer relationships, small group approaches, preaching, or teaching on critical areas.

Pastoral care has been explored in light of specific issues that young people face. One of these issues is sexuality, especially in the global context of expanding boundaries surrounding gender identity and sexual expression. In the African context, Ashamu's research explores pastoral care in light of LGBTIQA+ identity and sexuality issues among young people in South Africa.[17] This applies the work of pastoral care among young people who espouse different forms of sexual identification. Canales has explored how youth workers can effectively minister to young people who identify as trans in the North American and Roman Catholic context.[18] He boils down the

14. Patton, *Pastoral Care in Context*, 6.
15. Fowler, *Stages of Faith*, 20–21.
16. Best et al., "Pastoral Care," 125.
17. Ashamu, "Youth in South Africa."
18. Canales, *Ministry with LGBTQ Youth*.

approach to care, compassion, and empathy.[19] Although I would agree with Canales that youth ministries must seek to affirm the *imago dei* inherent in all human persons, including persons identifying as sexual minorities, it is critical to also consider the ministry of renewal into God's image that is part of Christian discipleship (2 Cor 3:18; Col 3:10). The ministry of Jesus Christ is that he invites human beings into a transformed life, through faith in him.

The HIV/AIDS pandemic in South Africa has also provided a critical reality of response by the church.[20] Baloyi has also explored the factors that foster the prevalence of Gender Based Violence (GBV) in African communities and its effects.[21] The most obvious is how this culture of violence and traumas that arise from it affect the children who grow up in such families. This entrenches oppressive views on womanhood, the abuse of drugs and alcohol that usually accompanies these acts of violence, and traumas that are definitive of those who have grown up under violent familial relationships. The COVID-19 pandemic has spotlighted these issues and provides the church with an important context for pastoral care.

Pastoral Care in the African Context

Magezi observes that the academic discourse on pastoral care in Africa is an emerging phenomenon.[22] Its "emergence" can be located in the often-complex cultural, historical, and religious contexts that face many African societies yet the modes and methods of pastoral care have developed in foreign contexts. Thus, a full-orbed pastoral care that is sensitive to the realities and needs within African societies must utilize the theological domains in light of social sciences as well as the porosity of culture.[23] Magezi lists African pastoral care theologians to include Masamba ma Mpolo (Democratic Republic of Congo); Emmanuel Y. Lartey (based in the United States but originally Ghana); Charles K. Konadu (Ghana); Wilhelmina J. Kalu and Daisy N. Nwachuku (Nigeria); Daniel J. Louw, Julian Müller, and Stephan de Beer (South Africa); Archiboldy Elifatio Lyimo and Derrick Lwekika (Tanzania); and Rose Zoé-Obianga (Cameroon).[24] Although the African

19. Canales, 252.
20. Bate, "Catholic Pastoral Care," 197–209.
21. Baloyi, "Wife Beating Amongst Africans," 1–10.
22. Magezi, "Pastoral Care in Africa," 1–7.
23. Mucherera and Lartey, *Counselling and Pastoral Care*.
24. Magezi, "Pastoral Care in Africa."

Association for Pastoral Studies and Counselling (AAPSC) was established in February 1985 in Limuru, Kenya, the lack of concerted efforts begs much more from African scholarship in this important area. Magezi also observes that the complexities of African life also serve as an impending obstacle in forging an "African" pastoral care approach.[25]

However, there is significant activity in pastoral care reflection in the African context. Mwangi explores the unique challenges of youth ministry in the PCEA (Kenya).[26] Akpanessien considers how pastoral care can be applied to the spiritual development of postmodern youth (Nigeria).[27] Magezi unpacks the decolonization of higher education and its implication for practical theology and pastoral care (South Africa).[28] Within the same country, Davies and Dreyer have also researched on the connection between pastoral care and domestic violence.[29] Nonetheless, there is a need to apply pastoral care reflection to particular issues in African youth life in East Africa and Kenya in particular. Bridging the divide between pastoral care discourse and practice that Magezi observes, this chapter seeks to focus on the pastoral responses in African youth ministry in light of the COVID-19 pandemic among youth leaders in Nairobi.[30]

A CASE STUDY OF PRESBYTERIAN CHURCH OF EAST AFRICA

The PCEA is a mission-founded church begun through the work of the missionary Rev. James Stewart and directors of the Imperial British East Africa (IBEA) chartered company, including Mr. A. L. Bruce among others. There work was carried out at the invitation of Sir William Mackinnon, beginning in 1891.[31] A mission station in Kibwezi would move to Kikuyu and Tumutumu missions through Rev. Thomas Watson in 1908 and to Chogoria in 1915. Through Act XVI of the 1936 General Assembly of the Church of Scotland Mission, the Oversees Presbytery of Kenya was formed to move it from the oversight of the Presbytery of East Africa. In 1945,

25. Magezi, "Pastoral Care in Africa," 3.
26. Mwangi, "Ministering to the Youth."
27. Akpanessien, "Postmodern Youth in Nigeria."
28. Magezi, "Public Pastoral Care," 1–10.
29. Davies and Dreyer, "Violence in South Africa."
30. Magezi, "Pastoral Care in Africa," 6.
31. PCEA, *Practice and Procedure*.

a formal partnership was entered with the Gospel Missionary Society at Kambui. The church has continued a consistent stream of Africanization of its mission work, with the Jitegemea Philosophy representative of the indigenization process in terms of its ministry work. The youth department was started in the 1960s in order to serve young people in and outside the church for holistic development. This section focuses on youth ministry in the PCEA and concludes that there is need to contextualize pastoral care theory and practice to African youth and for churches to develop youth policies that can enrich their pastoral workers to respond more holistically to the diverse youth pastoral care issues at hand.

The COVID-19 pandemic has created an intensified focus on the importance of pastoral care. More specifically, this section seeks to bridge the gap of academic discourse and practical ministry experience by bringing to the foreground practical experiences of youth workers in the ministry. This section presents data from the actual practices of pastoral care among youth pastors in the PCEA.[32] Beginning with semi-structured interviews, this section utilized a deductive methodology of categorizing the key themes and analyzing the same.[33] These first two activities are what constitute the descriptive-empirical and interpretive tasks according to Osmer's practical theological methodology.[34] The sections below engage in practical theological reflection, as it seeks to connect the emerging data with the theories. This last task includes the normative and pragmatic tasks according to Osmer and the "deductive-inductive" task according to Selvam.[35] These final tasks are what enrich the research questions and seek to offer a solution to the research problem identified.

Summary of Youth Ministry in PCEA

The youth pastors in the PCEA who participated in the research study represented the following nine parishes: PCEA Kahawa farmers, PCEA Ngong, PCEA Nairobi West, PCEA Kitengela, PCEA Happy Valley, PCEA Githunguri, PCEA Kirigiti, PCEA Uthiru, and PCEA Kabuku parishes. These parishes are representative of three different counties, including Nairobi, Kajiado, and Kiambu. I engaged in purposive sampling, focusing the

32. Selvam, *Empirical Research*, 72.
33. Selvam, *Empirical Research*, 78.
34. Osmer, *Practical Theology*.
35. Osmer, *Practical Theology*; Selvam, *Empirical Research*, 78.

research within the context of youth pastors in the PCEA youth pastors' network. Outside of the PCEA context, youth ministry in Africa continues to be a vibrant engagement in different denominational, theological, and practical ministry contexts. There are vibrant youth ministries in churches that identify as evangelical, those that identify as Pentecostal, as well as para-church ministries like Youth for Christ and Life Ministry Kenya, and other youth-serving organizations.

According to Figure 1 below, five of the youth pastors are aged between twenty-five and thirty-five years old and four of the youth pastors are aged above thirty-five years old. One youth pastor primarily serves the campus students cohort of youth ministry, whereas eight youth pastors serve the entire cohorts in youth ministry. These include teenagers (thirteen to eighteen years old), campus students (nineteen to twenty-four years old) and young professionals (twenty-five to thirty-five years old).

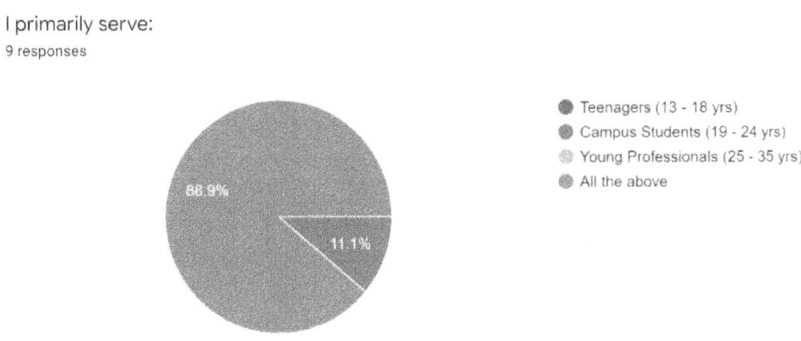

Figure 1: Youth Cohorts Served by the PCEA Youth Ministry

Figure 2 below unpacked the size of the youth ministries served by these youth pastors. According to the participants of the research, the size of the youth ministry served by the PCEA youth ministry is as follows:

- 77.8 percent serve a medium-sized youth ministry, that is, 100–250 youth.
- 11.1 percent serve a medium-to-large sized youth ministry, that is, 250–500 youth.
- 11.1 percent serve a large-sized youth ministry of 500+ youth.

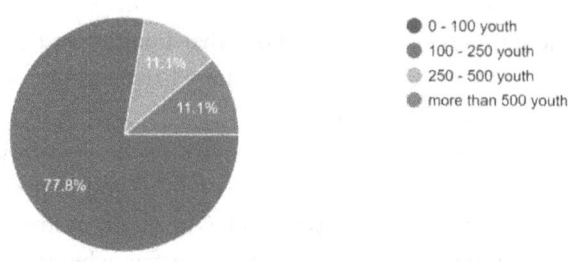

Figure 2: Size of the PCEA Youth Ministries in Local Churches

Challenges to Youth Ministry in Light of COVID

One of the questions was designed to measure the challenges that the youth pastors faced due to the pandemic. Using a Likert scale from zero (strongly disagree) to five (strongly agree), the results were as follows:

- A majority of the youth pastors (five out of nine, i.e., 55.6 percent) agreed that COVID-19 posed a challenge to their youth ministry, with two "agreeing" and three "strongly agreeing" that COVID-19 posed a challenge.

- A minority of the youth pastors (four out of nine, i.e., 44.4 percent) were neutral (i.e., selected "three" on the Likert scale) as to whether COVID presented a challenge to the youth ministry

The major challenges in the youth ministry as a result of COVID-19 from the youth pastors' observations can be summarized as follows:

- Reduced physical interactions
- Reduced service attendance
- Changes in life routines, e.g., educational progress[36]

---

36. The Ministry of Education in the 2020–2021 academic year made drastic changes in the educational programs in primary and secondary education, with holiday periods radically reduced to periods of one week in some cases in order to catch up with the normal routine of the public education system.

- Mental health issues
- Anxiety brought about by the changes
- Economic changes resulting in job losses, changes, and migrations

Online ministry was seen as one of the primary innovative responses of the time, though some raised the challenges of finances or the technological ability of the youth to access ministry programs. Because of the boundaries established by the Government and Ministry of Health (MOH) protocols, service attendance post-COVID has reduced in some churches. Those who were neutral concerning the impact of COVID-19 observed that though the pandemic brought challenges, it also expanded other opportunities for innovative ministry. Some of the platforms that have supported youth engagement in this season have included WhatsApp, Facebook, Instagram, and YouTube.

Emerging Issues in Post-COVID Youth Ministry

Since youth ministry is a contextual and practical theological approach to young people, then youth ministry post-COVID must grapple with the issues that emerged from the pandemic. The two major issues from the research concerning youth ministry include mental health and sexuality issues. Figure 3 below captures the critical areas of pastoral care according to the practical ministry of youth pastors in the wake of the pandemic:

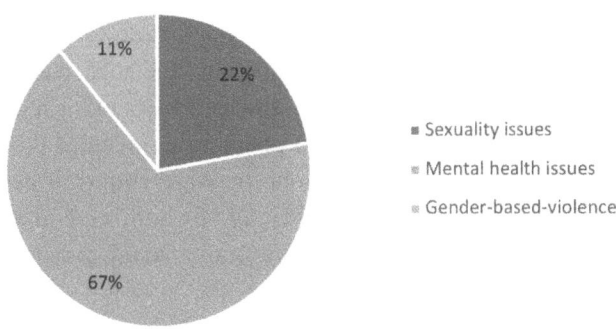

Figure 3: Emerging Issues in Youth Ministry in Light of COVID-19 Pandemic

Mental health has been compounded by the dramatic changes in life circumstances as well as the destabilizing effect that the pandemic has brought to young people's lives. With rising issues of anxiety about an unknown future and challenges in family support systems, young people have been greatly affected. One youth pastor also correlated the mental health issue with increased drugs and substance abuse due to idle time that young people had on their hands. Another youth pastor in the survey noted,

> A young person looks forward to a structured life; school for this number of years then *hustling* [looking for opportunities] or employment; when this structure is brought down and a new one created, many young people get anxious and desperate about their future leading to a number of mental issues.

This sentiment reveals how healthy transitions from adolescence into adulthood are critical markers of development among young people and their stakeholders. Because young people navigate significant questions in their journey towards adulthood, a significant change in their aspirations largely affects their well-being. Pastoral care is therefore a critical contributor to offering some level of structure and stability within a changing post-COVID context.

The sexuality issues were correlated to issues surrounding idle time, psychological coping, and sexually promiscuous behavior that led to pregnancy. Two youth pastors observed that some of the young people under their care were pregnant as a result of the changes brought about by COVID-19. These localized findings support the national research of teenage pregnancies in Kenya post-COVID. The Kenya Demographic Health Survey of 2014 estimated that one out of every five girls between the ages of fifteen and nineteen is reported to be pregnant or has already had a child.[37] From data collected in the study by the Population Council for the Presidential and Strategic Unit commissioned in June 2020, teenage pregnancy among girls aged between ten and nineteen years old is a critical issue.[38] The counties with the most teenage pregnancies included Kisumu (13 percent) followed by Kilifi, and Nairobi. In Wajir county, 9 percent of girls were pregnant or recently had a baby, all of whom were married.[39] Transactional sex was also a common issue among young girls who engaged in

---

37. Kenya National Bureau of Statistics, "Demographic and Health Survey," xxi.
38. Population Council, "Promises to Keep," 45.
39. Population Council, "Promises to Keep," 45.

sexual activities due to financial priorities in order to meet the needs of their home.[40]

Approaches in Pastoral Care

Pastoral care responses detail how the youth pastors have approached the challenges of the COVID-19 pandemic among their young people. These have included:

- Personal counseling—achieved through calls, prayers, and conversations
- Peer-to-peer counseling—achieved through initiating call-ministries and small groups among the young people
- Referrals—primarily to the parish minister (senior pastor) or other professionals, within and outside the congregation

The youth pastors noted the importance of biblical and professional counseling in helping young people deal with the realities brought about by the COVID-19 pandemic. In fact, some suggested that churches should equip the youth pastors and other youth leaders with counseling skills. Several youth pastors also noted the importance of parental involvement in the well-being of the young people. Others observed that youth-inclusive leadership can help to bring young people closer to the church and help them both to serve and be served by the church's holistic ministries.

RETHINKING PASTORAL CARE

African Worldviews in Pastoral Care Giving

Whereas this chapter sought to engage pastoral care issues within the context of youth ministry in the wake of the COVID-19 pandemic, pastoral care is still located within a postcolonial context. Branson observes how communities of faith in the Bible are always crossing boundaries and how that necessitates sensitive listening and discernment of other people's perspectives and situations.[41] He considers God's instructions to the exilic community during Jeremiah's prophetic timeline (Jer 29:7), the inclusivity

---

40. Population Council, "Promises to Keep," 49.
41. Branson, "Multicultural Initiatives," 33–58.

of the immigrant in Old Testament Law (Deut 10:19; Lev 19:33–34), and God's commissioning in the book of Jonah for the prophet to give witness to Nineveh.[42] Within the New Testament, Branson considers the multicultural underpinnings of the Acts of the apostles through his reflection:

> Bicultural Hellenistic Jews and Jewish converts were included—but what about Gentiles? Scripture names bicultural persons who played key roles (Moses, Ruth, Paul, Timothy) and Gentiles who are included in the Jewish lineage (Tamar, Rahab, Bathsheba). But how is the church to understand its own social composition?[43]

Similar tensions color contemporary Christian engagement and pastoral care within pluralistic societies such as can be found in many African cities. Thus, even within this specific case of pastoral care in youth ministry in Africa, there is need to consider different voices and how they may shed light on the pastoral care concerns in such contextual cases.[44]

Ramsay further perceives the need for reflexive interlocution between practical experience and theoretical bases.[45] This interlocution falls within the domain of practical theology, which has methodologically served this purpose of engaging how specific knowledge domains interact with praxis, and vice versa, and their attention to particular audiences.[46] Magezi speaks from the South African context and interacts with global practical theologians, noting the nuanced emphases as well as trajectories among scholars such as Dreyer, Muller, and Osmer.[47] This means that, in our specific case, youth ministry practice can and should inform pastoral care theory, and that the canons of pastoral care must be in touch with issues affecting young people. This is further engaged in the next section.

Lastly, a postcolonial turn considers the salience of African spirituality and how it is interconnected with all facets of life for those cared for.[48] Thus, pastoral care within the African context is never merely a "pastoral" or even a "spiritual" undertaking, but it often engages the linkages between the individual and her community, her sociocultural context, as well as her

---

42. Branson, "Multicultural Initiatives," 36.
43. Branson, "Multicultural Initiatives," 36.
44. Ramsay, *Pastoral Theology and Care*, 88.
45. Ramsay, *Pastoral Theology and Care*, 89.
46. Magezi, "Practical Theology in Africa," 119.
47. Magezi, "Practical Theology in Africa."
48. Ramsay, *Pastoral Theology and Care*, 92; Masango, "African Spirituality," 931.

religious and cultural orientations.[49] These issues are the *homo africanus*, defined by the Congolese practical theologian Masamba ma Mpolo as the sanctity of life, the relationships between illness, misfortune, and sin, and the place of elders and the spirit world in African thought.[50] This is the same observation by Acolatse, that African cultural worldview and cosmology is foundational in African pastoral care.[51] From the research, it was evident that the youth issues faced occur within the ecosystem of community. Young people expect structure and understanding from their guardians, as well as a smooth transition into a future that supports their well-being. Pastoral care givers should therefore invite those they care for into a full-orbed introspection and consideration of a multiplicity of factors that are critical in their unconscious self-perception and in how they live in the real world.

For the case of teenage pregnancies, for example, pastoral care givers must gently probe ongoing issues in the families of origin, the economic stresses that may inform sexual expression, as well as the person's values that are informed by their faith. The research revealed that the increase in sexual activity could be correlated with the stresses and strains brought about by retrogressed educational progress as well as the heightened tensions in the home as a result of changes in the economic livelihoods of the parents.[52] However, these are not only engaged from a humanistic perspective, but within the full scope of a Christian worldview—including aspects to do with Christian anthropology, hamartiology, soteriology, and Christology. Therefore, pastoral care within the African context necessitates a holistic approach.

Taking Youth Issues Head On

Pastoral care in the Christian context is grounded within the Judeo-Christian worldview, informed by biblical revelation, and attendant to real issues that people face. The significance of this point is that pastoral care must not only be conversant with the African context at large but also on the lived realities of young people. In the African continent, young people comprise a large population. Therefore, ministry engagement by the church to the society must be geared towards young people. Pastoral care in Africa must

---

49. Ramsay, *Pastoral Theology and Care*, 93.
50. Magezi, "Practical Theology in Africa," 133.
51. Acolatse, *For Freedom or Bondage?*
52. Population Council, "Promises to Keep."

attend to the unique issues that face African youth, including navigating identity issues, sexuality issues, and socioeconomic issues.

The first issue is the question of African identity among African youth. Mucherera observes how young people within the Shona communities in Zimbabwe wrestle with the question of identity as they navigate traditional cultural worldviews and postmodernity. Several scholars have extrapolated similar observations of this "hybridity" in cultural belonging among young people in different geographical (Kenya) and religious contexts (Muslim youth in North Korea).[53] The same trajectory could be traced among urban Kenyan youths who oscillate between a variety of cultural and religious contexts. This "cultural refugeeism" leads to a hybridization of cultures, and fragmentation of African youth cultural constructs with consequential issues for their overall well-being.[54]

Part of how this cultural fragmentation affects young people is in the area of their spiritual formation as it pertains to concepts such as gender, sexuality, mental health, and vocation. Setran and Kiesling explore how, for example, youth care givers must enable young people to explore questions of identity within a safe community, expand their visions of vocational discernment beyond the materialistic ethos that influences their perceptions of "a well-paying job," and help them develop a big picture "theology of sexuality" that undergirds its anthropology, soteriology, and eschatology—that sexuality is a good gift of God, to be used for the nourishing bonds of marriage and family and to be enjoyed as a time-bound gift with eternal ramifications.[55]

These pointers are relevant for pastoral care within the new realities that COVID-19 has brought about. Many youth ministers in the research acknowledged how COVID-19 has affected the sexuality of young people as well as the vocational restlessness resulting from a stuttering educational system, shut down in phases as part of the government's COVID-19 response directives. Pastoral care must seek to reconcile those who feel alienated from God due to pregnancy and also speak wisely to those wrestling with sexual identity questions. On the other hand, pastoral care givers within the youth ministry context have an opportunity to explore the core questions of vocation—moving beyond the "Kenyan dream" of getting good grades in basic education; maintaining a stellar performance in secondary education; garnering a high-flying course usually limited to the "vocational trinity" of

---

53. O'Connor, "Everyday Hybridity," 250–72; Karanja, "'Homeless' at Home."
54. Mucherera, *Counseling and Pastoral Care*; Ugor, "Extenuating Circumstances," 2.
55. Setran and Kiesling, *Spiritual Formation*, 79, 112, 189.

engineer, doctor, or lawyer; and beginning a family and proverbially "living happily ever after." Given the reality of salary cuts and job losses that have affected many, pastoral care givers are invited to help young people explore vocation from within the intersections of their unique personalities, the needs around them and in the world, and the providential opportunities before them, as well as how such vocational undertakings influence and impact their views on a successful life, the responsibilities of family life, and one's service to the church and society.[56] Forster observes the necessity of a theology of vocation to engage the dualism often presented between faith and work.[57] Pastoral care in African youth ministry post-COVID is a tremendous call to reconsider our theology of work or vocation.

In summary, the COVID-19 pandemic has led to migrations and mobilities, not only in educational systems but also in socioeconomic contexts and geographic contexts. All these factors transform how we view Christian ministry in general and pastoral care in particular. Pastoral care givers in the context of African youth ministry must negotiate a variety of issues with divine tact, careful listening, wise discernment, and contextual sensitivity that helps them to walk alongside their young people in a helpful manner. Part of what this task entails is connecting young people with other networks of care and opportunity, so as to ensure their holistic wellbeing. In the context of the local congregation, this may entail equipping parents with the tools of adolescent care giving, connecting recent graduates with mid-level to senior-level managers for career or business mentorship, and also connecting those with mental health challenges with Christian counselors and psychologists in the communities of faith. This is the kind of intergenerational approach that can strengthen the church's ministry to care for her young.[58]

Churches That Nurture Healthy Care Givers

The final issue that this chapter revealed is that pastoral caregiving is dependent on the pastoral care giver themselves. Thus, the COVID-19 pandemic unveils the need to develop policies as well as educational opportunities for the onboarding, development, and deployment of healthy youth ministers. Within the Kenyan context, several policy frameworks have been developed

---

56. Setran and Kiesling, *Spiritual Formation*, 136.
57. Forster, "Nature of Work," 7.
58. Chiroma, "Intergenerational Issues," 360–62.

to ensure smooth transitions of young people into adulthood and the responsibilities that come along with it. The Kenya Youth Development Policy (2019) was rolled out by the Kenyan Government for the purpose of strengthening the lives of young people in line with the African Union Agenda 2063, UN Strategy for the Youth (2014), and Sustainable Development Goals (2030). Given the fact that churches minister to young people, how can they have relevant policies to guide their philosophies of youth ministries and their development of youth leaders and youth pastors? Within the South African context, Aziz has explored this gap and offered various solutions to how the office of youth pastor can be developed.[59]

This chapter revealed that youth ministers acknowledge the need to build relevant skills and knowledge that can help them in offering holistic pastoral care. What this means is that churches must develop guidelines, not only on their youth engagement in ministry, but also concerning their youth pastors or youth workers.[60] Within the PCEA, the youth ministry has been in existence since the 1960s. Began through the frontier efforts of Anna and Jerry Bedford, it is now overseen by an ordained minister in the youth department in the head office.[61] The *Practice and Procedure* manual, contains the framework for the church's ministry, including how local churches (parishes) run their youth fellowships.[62] While ordained ministers have a scheme of service that outlines their terms of engagement, youth workers are engaged on different terms based on a need-by-need approach from the local churches. What this means is that there is no standardization of onboarding, retention, development, and deployment of youth workers in the context of a local church. Some churches, particularly in urban centers, may have well-defined policies, but clearly there is a need to develop an overarching policy of engaging youth workers, coordinators, and pastors, depending on how churches define them. Fortunately, the PCEA has

---

59. Aziz et al., "Career Youth Pastor."

60. Within Kenyan churches, those who have oversight over youth ministries are defined in different ways. Some are lay leaders, whereas some are ordained. Some serve in a voluntary capacity, while others serve in a paid capacity. They are also given different terms such as "youth director" or "youth coordinator." Some of them specialize only in the organizing, administration, and implementation of youth ministry activities as it pertains to youth, whereas others serve additional roles such as children pastors or leaders as well as evangelists within the context of the PCEA.

61. PCEA, *Practice and Procedure*, 328; On the stories of Anna and Jerry Bedford as frontier missionaries, see Focer, "Frontier Interns Reenvisioned Missions"; Focer, "Frontier Internship in Mission."

62. PCEA, *Practice and Procedure*, 328.

mandated a committee to work on a possible framework for engaging its youth pastors. This has ramifications on pastoral caregiving as there is a correlation between the holistic development of youth care givers and the quality of their care giving.

WAY FORWARD

This chapter surveyed the existing literature in pastoral care, particularly within the African context. By so doing, the study explored different models and issues in pastoral care within the continent. More specifically, this chapter study engaged the lacuna in utilizing an empirical approach of pastoral care in youth ministry theory and praxis. By interviewing nine youth pastors in the PCEA in three counties in Kenya, this chapter explored the emerging themes in pastoral care that are affecting young people. This chapter revealed that two key emerging issues in the wake of the COVID-19 pandemic are sexuality and mental health issues, although I expanded my practical theological reflection in the discussion to include the concept of African identity and vocation given how COVID-19 has impacted employment in the country. Considering the empirical data in light of the literature in pastoral care, this chapter explored three key issues that arise in light of the qualitative study. First, there is a need to embed an African epistemology in pastoral care—this includes issues as diverse as considering the communality of African societies and how this influences pastoral issues. Secondly, there is a need to contextualize pastoral care in theoretical reflection and ministry practice to the lives of African young people. Lastly, this chapter explored how the development of policy frameworks within ecclesial institutions can enrich the quality of pastoral care givers in youth ministry and, by extension, strengthen the church's ministry to her young people.

7

Nurturing a Politically Engaged Faith

IN THE DAYS LEADING up to Kenya's August 9, 2022 elections, the race for the gubernatorial seat for the country's capital—between the sitting senator Johnson Sakaja and Polycarp Igathe, former deputy governor and reputable business leader—was hotly debated. Their contestation was premised on the provision of better healthcare, water, and sanitation and better land management and developmental policies that would safeguard the livelihoods of residents of Nairobi. Perhaps the most critical demographic that such policies directly affect are Kenya's young people. The Kenyan Constitution defines young people as those from the age of eighteen to thirty-five years old.[1] The Kenya Youth Development Policy is the policy document that charts a comprehensive vision for the well-being and sustainable human development of this critical demographic. This chapter also focuses on political youth participation, which Kenya Youth Development Policy defines as in the following way:

> Youth having influence on and shared responsibility for decisions and actions that affect the lives of the youth within a context that acknowledges and respects their talents and strengths and supports them in finding ways to deal with the issues that affect them.[2]

---

1. State Department for Youth, "Youth Development Policy," xi.
2. State Department for Youth, "Youth Development Policy," xii.

While this is an aspirational goal that Kenya's development agenda seeks to achieve, this chapter investigates the role of the church in the discipleship of young people towards this public agenda. The available evidence reveals that disinterest in political affairs among young people is growing. For instance, registered voters among eligible young people (eighteen to thirty-five years old) stands at 39.84 percent of registered voters, a 5.27 percent decline from the 2007 elections, with a greater decrease among females (7.75 percent) than males (2.89 percent).[3] With the total voters standing at 22,120,458 Kenyans, the youth who have registered to vote are 8,812,791. This presents an interesting problem statistically. If we take the 2021 population estimates by various sources to stand at 54,985,698, then assuming that the youth population (eighteen to thirty-five years old) is 29 percent of total population, eligible youth voters in 2022 stand at 15,945,853.[4] Given only 8,812,791 registered for voting (55.27 percent), then 44.73 percent of youth will not be voting. This voter apathy may be only one indicator of the lack of youth agency in the country's political processes.

The intersection of church and politics remains a contested yet an important terrain for discussion. While some Christians and theologians may be averse to the topic of politics, in many African states the consequences of negative politics quickly disabuses us from such an explicit dichotomy. Boyo argues that a familiarization with the African worldview is necessary in bridging the gap between church and politics as it seeks to offer a holistic cosmology that eschews dichotomous thinking.[5] In Kenya, the church has had a multipronged approach to various political dispensations—from the pre-colonial missionary interaction with African traditional religions, to the church's responses to post-colonial African political leadership and the various struggles for freedom in various countries in SSA. Since politics has to do with matters of negotiating power for the common good of citizens, as Innes defines it, then the church as the pillar of truth, justice, and righteousness functions as a voice of conscience for the activities of the state.[6]

Within the literature, various political participation processes include voter turnout, political protests, and collective actions as well as participating in community activities.[7] These scholars also note that patterns of politi-

---

3. Chebukati, "Media Briefing."
4. AFIDEP, "Kenya Briefing Note"; Nyakwara, "State of Kenya Population."
5. Boyo, *Church and Politics*, 5.
6. Innes, *Christ and the Kingdoms*, 181.
7. Resnick and Casale, "Participation of African Youth," 2.

cal participation among urban African youth are similar to other regions of the globe. Kimari also observes how the theorization of youth as a socially constructed phenomenon needs to pay attention to the historical antecedents between youth and the state in Kenya.[8] For example, they observe that young people have played a critical role in the calls for societal change, and this can be seen through the Mau Mau rebellion (Kenya Land and Reform Army), which was championed by young Kikuyu men, as well as the political hand over to young, educated Kenyans during independence. Youth movements, such as the contemporary Mombasa Republican Council (MRC) and al-Shabab (meaning "youth" in Arabic), are understood as political responses to "secessionist struggles" handed down across generations and revealing the tensions between generational factors, state suppression, and youth political agency that intertwines human rights, vigilante groups, and militant approaches in political contexts.[9] Generational differences in political participation between young people and older generations have been attributed to different cultural ideals. Older generations are more sensitive to economic well-being, religious affiliations, as well as orderly political processes. Younger generations, within a postmodern cultural milieu, are more skeptical of institutions, and more skewed towards "post-materialist goals" such as social justice, equity, and personal freedom.[10] Following this argument, one may infer that within Kenyan politics, which is still largely ethnic based, young people are weary of such political narratives and are passive towards any political interventions.

On the other hand, the role of religion in political participation has taken two different routes. One extreme has been the role of religion in fostering political violence, terrorism, as well as ethnic cleansing. However, some scholars have taken note of how Islam is viewed as a violent religion, thereby fostering more entrenched conflict in plural societies.[11] Such a critical approach considers the conflicting ways in which religion, and even Christianity, has been used to subjugate people through politicization of religion. The second route considers the positive role that religion has played within political processes. For instance, Kritzinger notes the role of the missionary enterprise in developing schools and hospitals, and Sabar

---

8. Kimari et al., "Youth, the Kenyan State," 695.
9. Kimari et al., "Youth, the Kenyan State," 695.
10. Resnick and Casale, "Participation of African Youth," 3.
11. Mohamed, "Youth Negotiating Political Agency," 305.

has noted the role of the church—in independent Kenya in the second liberation movement—with the launching of multi-party politics.[12]

Reflectively, while young people may not reveal specific political interventions or actions, their opinions towards leaders who pursue a new narrative of issue-based politics continues to increase, particularly within social media mobilization as well as the everyday narratives of young people.[13] This thesis is supported by the Arab Spring uprising of the 2010s in the Middle East and North Africa as well as the revolutionary youth movements within the higher education spaces in South Africa in the last decade. Exploring the role of social media in the Arab Spring, Comunello and Anzera observe that social media has thus arisen as a unique site of political mobilization based on its ability to offer a "networked individualism" and sense of agency, while at the same time contributing an uncanny ability to support grassroots action within a digital subculture.[14] Others have noted the role of social media in raising awareness on poverty issues through higher education reforms by analyzing the 2015 #FeesMustFall movement and their contribution to national political discourses.[15] These scholars note the saliency of new media and their transformation of traditional protest activities in offering new ways to communicate and participate in what they term as "informational activism." While political actors may not listen to the constructive voices of young people, what digital spaces offer is a sense of inclusivity by functioning as a youth subculture.[16]

The role of the internet and social media in the political agency of several African countries such as Ethiopia, Uganda, and Zimbabwe, among others, has been explored.[17] In his research on Kenyan youth political agency among six hundred university students, Kamau observes that while youth may not have participated in physical civic duties, a majority of them had come across public campaigns via social media, with a significant number participating in sharing the campaigns via digital means.[18] Okoth's survey of how Kenyans on Twitter (KOT) use visuals as a way of political participation reveals the salience of social media for both social networking

12. Kritzinger, "Church and Development"; Sabar, *Church, State, and Society*, 3.
13. Kamau, "Democratic Engagement," 130.
14. Comunello and Anzera, "Will the Revolution be Tweeted," 468.
15. Bosch, "Twitter and Participatory Citizenship," 159–73.
16. Olagunju et al., "Beyond #FeesMustFall," 10.
17. Mutsvairo, *Digital Activism*.
18. Kamau, "Engaged Online," 126.

and collective action.[19] The argument made is that while young people may not reveal increasing face-to-face political engagements, the digital space is offering them a new way for taking up political agency. However, some critique these social media political mobilizations as mainly based on class politics, especially among the rising a Kenyan middle class that lacks correlative outputs in tangible action or material democratic activities.[20] Whatever the case, the church has a role in helping young people take political agency in public life through actual mobilizations and action.

PRIVATE OR PUBLIC? THE GAP OF DISCIPLESHIP

This chapter situates the discussion of building political agency among young people through the ministry of the church in Kenya. The problem statement is that the church has not discipled her young people to participate in public life and citizenship. Given the fact that Christianity plays a critical role in the public space, it is important to explore the contribution of the church in Kenya in holistic discipleship of young people for public participation. The current practice of discipleship can be termed a "privatized" discipleship that is anchored on a sacred-secular divide, inherent within dichotomized worldviews inherited from the Western intellectual heritage. This chapter will retrieve a more holistic vision for discipleship from the theologian Dietrich Bonhoeffer as well as the political theology of Timothy Njoya to explore political participation among young people.

THE INHERITED DISCIPLESHIP MODELS

Youth work in Kenya has developed as an offshoot of the evangelical youth movements in North America. These North American youth discipleship movements took the form of Fellowship of Christian Unions (FOCUS), registered in Kenya in 1973, and Kenya Youth for Christ (KYFC) in 1975. FOCUS is affiliated with the International Fellowship of Evangelical Students (IFES), the National Council of Churches of Kenya (NCCK), and the Evangelical Alliance of Kenya (EAK).[21] The KYFC is affiliated to the Youth

---

19. Okoth, "Kenyans on Twitter," 2.

20. Burbidge, "'Middle Class Zone,'" 208; Mukhongo, "Participatory Media Cultures," 151; Ogola, "#Whatwouldmagufulido?"

21. Focus Kenya, "49th FOCUS AGM."

for Christ movement. What is significant from the formation of these youth discipleship movements is not only that their dates are close to each other but perhaps that they were precipitated by the Lausanne International Congress for World Evangelization held in 1974. Kirkpatrick views the key contribution of the Congress as a critique of imperial and hegemonic approaches to evangelization, as well as the contribution of key Global South leaders, specifically Rene Padilla and his construal of "integral mission."[22] This view of discipleship and mission was anchored in the expansion of the gospel vision, not only to the privatized journey of Christians to heaven but also to the liberation of their sociopolitical contexts. Thus, evangelical discourse in the Global South led to the mushrooming of more publicly engaged Christian ministries, and to the rise of postcolonial discourses that respond to Western hegemony.[23] An argument that Padilla and other theologians from the Global South have made is that Christian discipleship must engage the contexts that Christians find themselves in. It must be conceded that the vision of discipleship among young people in Kenya was anchored on the sacred-secular divide that narrows down the Christian vision only to conversion and not to sanctification or to the attendant transformation of personal life and public transformation.

Ward traces the roots of evangelical youth work to the nineteenth century.[24] Similarly, the practical theologian Andrew Root argues that the modern practice of youth ministry, particularly in its obsession with age segregation, is hinged on an idealization of "youthfulness," which is a recent development of the twentieth century.[25] He observes that this "obsession" is rooted in the last one hundred years of "technological, geopolitical, and religious" transitions. Ward is incisive in noting the sociopolitical context that shaped the youth movement, exploring the impact of the World Wars in creating anxiety through the Great Depression of the 1930s that led to a preference of consumerist capitalism as the economic solution of the time. Given this cultural context, Root argues that organizations such as Young Life and Youth for Christ were innovations that were focused on engaging the middle-class youth coming out of this socioeconomic context.[26] North American youth ministry, contextually understood, was a response to the

22. Kirkpatrick, "Origins of Integral Mission."
23. Kirkpatrick, *Gospel for the Poor*, 31.
24. Ward, *Growing Up Evangelical*.
25. Root, *Faith Formation*, 17.
26. Root, *Faith Formation*, 29.

sociopolitical context of North America and the issues unique to that time and place.

Ward's history of youth ministry reaches further back.[27] YMCA traces its history to 1844, when George Williams and friends gathered for the first YMCA meeting with the purpose of equipping young men to evangelize neighbors through prayer meetings and Bible studies. In 1883, William Smith began the Boy's Brigade in Glasgow. Baden-Powell (founder of the Boy Scouts of America) was less enthusiastic about the Boy's Brigade and its evangelistic or militaristic stance. In 1888, the first church-based youth ministry program called the *International Christian Endeavour Society* was started by Francis Clark, a minister in Maine, who was invited by the Sunday School Union. The main emphasis of youth work was mission.

Senter historically observes four phases of youth ministry in the context of North America: 1824–1875, 1881–1925, 1933–1989, and the 1990s onwards.[28] The first phase (1824–1875) focused on the social issues facing young people and was concerned about changing the outward lifestyle of young people. This phase was championed by Christian societies and organizations that have already been mentioned such as Sunday schools, YMCA, and juvenile temperance societies. The second phase (1881–1925) took on an educational emphasis in line with the developing theory of progressive education. The third phase (1933–1989) served as a corrective to the waning emphasis on God's presence, was more relational, and converged on the Great Commission and the Great Commandment. The fourth phase, according to Senter, is concerned with navigating the pluralistic culture of contemporary societies.[29]

Since most discipleship movements of young people can be traced to the third phase, one sees how these movements were entrenched in a sacred-secular divide whose main emphasis was the first experience of salvation—conversion—instead of participating in the new life that salvation brings. This dichotomy has not helped young people engage with sociocultural issues unique in their time. These issues include participating in the scientific dialogues taking place in the society, the intersection of the gospel and African traditional religions and cultures, as well as the Christian view of political engagement, particularly within political states that are marked more by authoritarian approaches of politics and where

27. Ward, *Growing Up Evangelical*.
28. Senter, *Four Views*, xii.
29. Senter, *Four Views*, xiii.

corruption, ethnocentrism, and hampered development are core realities of many African countries.

In the recent literature, evangelical theology, particularly in its nationalistic and state-imperialist streams signified during the US Trump era, has received several critiques.[30] The strength of the evangelical tradition may be its activism, conversionism, cruciformity, and bibliocentricity—the so called "quadrilateral" championed by Bebbington.[31] However, if these emphases do not aim at personal and public transformation, then they may be used for selfish agenda. No wonder postcolonial theology in Africa focused theological reflection on social issues, rather than questions of truth or epistemology, as a way of restoring dignity to the experiences of societies within the Global South, often in the wake of domination.[32] This chapter explores the theologies of Dietrich Bonhoeffer, as well as the Kenyan theologian and Presbyterian church leader Timothy Njoya, as a way of retrieving a theological underpinning for political engagement that pays attention to the Kenyan political context and agency of young people. The choice of Bonhoeffer is to show how even a lauded figure in evangelical theology can be read as one who engaged in contextual theology. The choice of Njoya is a case study of an African theologian grappling with his political context.

BONHOEFFER AS A MODEL OF HOLISTIC YOUTH DISCIPLESHIP

Bonhoeffer, the German pastor-theologian who was born in 1906 and died in 1945, was so concerned for the church's germaneness for his sociocultural situation that he posed the following questions: "What did Jesus want to say to us? What does he want from us today?"[33] By beginning his theological reflection here, Bonhoeffer exemplifies how following Jesus Christ is immersed in contemporary issues. Such radical following of Jesus frees people from the constrictions of worldly domination and empowers them for holistic discipleship. In his own words,

> Only where Jesus' entire commandment and the call to unlimited discipleship remain intact are persons fully free to enter into Jesus'

30. Aziz, "Public Practical Theology," 4.

31. Aziz, "Public Practical Theology," 4; Vanhoozer and Treier, *Mirror of Scripture*, 27.

32. Sakupapa, "Decolonising Content"; Smith et al., *Evangelical Postcolonial Conversations*, 14.

33. Bonhoeffer, *Discipleship*, 21.

community. Those who follow Jesus' commandment entirely, who let Jesus' yoke rest on them without resistance, will find the burdens they must bear to be light. In the gentle pressure of this yoke, they will receive the strength to walk the right path without becoming weary.[34]

Rightly so, Bonhoeffer here together with Ogden, contend that discipleship is centered on the public ministry of Christ and his proclamation of the kingdom of God, which affects all spheres of life.[35] Bonhoeffer's "cost of discipleship" was complicated by his unlawful imprisonment.[36] From his reflections in this prison experience, one hears the cries often offered by African youths who navigate marginal contexts: "Every available alternative seemed equally intolerable, repugnant, and futile." Bonhoeffer's context was in Nazi-occupied Germany where he was faced daily with the harsh realities of hatred, evil, and suffering, thereby stimulating his reflections on how Christ could be present in the midst of such a broken world.[37] He was accused of conspiring to kill Hitler, a reality that saw him executed as a martyr.[38] In Bonhoeffer's view, the Christian task in such circumstances is not merely "waiting and looking" but "sympathy and action, not in the first place by his own sufferings, but by the sufferings of his brethren, for whose sake Christ suffered."[39] Therefore, Bonhoeffer here ties his political activism to the ministry of Jesus Christ, particularly his suffering, not merely as a fact to be believed but a reality to be lived out.

Van der Westhuizen, in consideration of Bonhoeffer's sacrifice, wrestles with how this may apply to the church in many of our pluralistic and secular societies.[40] To begin, just as Bonhoeffer proffers, we are reminded that the church must always be cruciform in shape—living in light of the resurrection power in the midst of a broken world and sharing this hope with our neighbors. Our faith that justifies us must never be bereft of any real transformation. Bonhoeffer models for us what faith formation, in particular discipleship, looks like in the turmoil of the world. Perhaps young people have not taken the church with the seriousness it deserves because

---

34. Bonhoeffer, *Discipleship*, 29.
35. Ogden, "Discipleship Deficit," 2.
36. Bonhoeffer, *Letters and Papers from Prison*, 3.
37. Van der Westhuizen, "Bonhoeffer's Question," 147.
38. Metaxas, *Bonhoeffer*.
39. Bonhoeffer, *Letters and Papers from Prison*, 14.
40. Van der Westhuizen, "Bonhoeffer's Question," 161.

it has not articulated such a radical "cost of discipleship" that empties itself of power-plays and considers afresh God's working in the marginalized spaces.[41] Bonhoeffer's life intimates that during the "religionless Christianity" of his time, he offered young people the substance of the faith—Root's thesis, noting Bonhoeffer's Sunday school teaching in Harlem, for example, is that Bonhoeffer's ministry to young people between 1925 and 1939 offers a model for how youth minsters might make the "theological turn," by participating in God's action in the lives of children and youth.[42] Metaxas also notes Bonhoeffer's invitation of young people to the church in his lectures to his students, where one of them records,

> He [Bonhoeffer] pointed out that nowadays we often ask ourselves whether we still need God. But this question, he said, is wrong. We are the ones who are questioned. The Church exists and God exists, and we are asked whether we are willing to be of service, for God needs us.[43]

Here we see Bonhoeffer's concern to deeply engage young people. His engagement, we learn, went beyond the intellectual exploration of questions of young people to their real lives. We learn that Bonhoeffer invited young people to his parent's home—sidelining the dichotomy between the private "Christian life" and the more public "family life"—inviting them to musical concerts and even to the "nearby *Bierkeller.*"[44] Another method of youth discipleship that Bonhoeffer exemplifies is the art of retreating for the purpose of catechetical instruction through scripture meditation and spiritual conversations.[45] More remarkably, and closer to our African context of sociocultural breakdown and economic chaos, Bonhoeffer's ministry (teaching confirmation class) to the marginalized youth at *Zionskirche* in Wedding, Berlin, reveals further his ministerial acumen and Christian discipleship.[46] Shortly after his ordination on November 15, 1931, the young pastor is sent to replace an older minister in discipling rowdy youths. He wins their hearts through connecting storytelling with the eschatological hope of Scripture, both a contextual and conservative approach to ministry that endeared the hearts of these young people to him.

41. Smit, "Reception of Bonhoeffer," 102.
42. Dean and Root, *Theological Turn*, 19.
43. Metaxas, *Bonhoeffer*, 125.
44. Metaxas, *Bonhoeffer*, 126–27.
45. Metaxas, *Bonhoeffer*, 129.
46. Metaxas, *Bonhoeffer*, 130–37.

He would go on to do home visits, and the tone of his message during their confirmation on March 13, 1932, reveals how much he had struck a chord with them—his invitation of them to communion showed that even this towering theologian and budding pastor was concerned for young people. In essence, Bonhoeffer models an incarnational approach to youth discipleship, an approach that meets them where they are, reminiscing his theology of incarnation that he so eloquently proposes in his *Discipleship*:

> The Body of Christ takes up space on earth. That is the consequence of the Incarnation. Christ came into his own. But at his birth they gave him a manger, for "there was no room in the inn." At his death they thrust him out, and his Body hung between earth and heaven on the gallows. But despite all this, the Incarnation does involve a claim to a space of its own on earth. Anything which claims space is visible. Hence the Body of Christ can only be a visible body, or else it is not a Body at all.[47]

Bonhoeffer's language of the church as a tangible body of Christ models what Root calls "relational youth ministry," which borrows a lot from the pastor-theologian's practical theology that is grounded in real life realities—and that calls for public transformation.[48] Part of this transformation was his alliance with the Confessing Church, which rejected the antisemitism of the pro-Nazi, Protestant, and state church of his time. His radical discipleship would eventually cost him his life. Bonhoeffer's discipleship was, therefore, public out of necessity. This chapter desires to arouse scholars and practitioners working with young people on the necessity of bridging this private-public divide in discipleship for the transformation of our African societies today and tomorrow.

TIMOTHY NJOYA'S POLITICAL THEOLOGY

Timothy Njoya (c. 1941–present), together with other Kenyan theologians and clerics such as Henry Okullu (c. 1929–1999) and Alexander Muge (c. 1948–1990), both of the Anglican Church of Kenya, as well as the Roman Catholic priest John Kaiser (c. 1932–2000), played prominent roles in the political process of the country. Their lives reveal an understanding of the Christian life, not only as a private religion but as a way of life that has

---

47. Bonhoeffer, *Discipleship*, 223.
48. Root, *Relational Youth Ministry*.

consequences for public life. Bongmba observes that these religious leaders viewed their ministry, particularly their preaching ministry, as an expository application of Jesus' public ministry in response to some of the political suppressions of the time, including restricted freedoms, free speech, and a hashed opposition that would be an important agenda for the National Council of Churches of Kenya (NCCK).[49] Njoya's autobiography, *We the People: Thinking Heavenly, Acting Kenyanly*, offers us a vantage point into Njoya's primary preoccupation. Njoya observes that the state politics of his time viewed Kenyans as property in a market rather than creatures of God created with some level of sovereignty.[50] This agenda of "transformation" was a departure from his contemporaries' narratives of a "successful life." A case in point of the integral view of discipleship, which fermented in postcolonial discourse of the last half of the twentieth century, is seen in Njoya's intellectual appreciation of Paulo Freire's *Pedagogy of the Oppressed*. He applies this to the enduring colonial machinery and its intersectionality with poverty, education, and religion:

> The engine of the success narrative began with slavery, then became urbanized and industrialized into colonialism. Colonialism masqueraded as independence for the good, stability and profitability of the market. The same church whose catechism taught me in Sunday School that God created children as sovereign, with a moral consciousness and divine responsibility, collaborated with the market to build schools that would grade children according to their market value. Instead of equipping children with democratic values and social skills to build a multicultural and equal society, education created two societies: the top class of the privileged, totalitarian, and parasitical few who owned and consumed everything, and the bottom majority that produced everything and ate nothing. As a system of broken material relationships, Kenya could not maintain social order without excessive use of force, as was codified in the Lancaster Constitution and embodied in the one-party totalitarian state.[51]

For Njoya, such intellectual reflections were not merely ivory-tower discourses detached from everyday life but embedded within a politically engaged life in the church-state relationships of the democratic process of multipartyism. I have drawn the parallel between Njoya's political theology

---

49. Bongmba, *Handbook of African Theology*, 8.
50. Njoya, *We the People*, 30.
51. Njoya, *We the People*, 22.

and Okullu's, along with their contributions to African political theology and contemporary Christian life.[52] But in Njoya's thinking, one can trace how a conflation of the church with the state prevents the church from offering an objective moral voice to the political ills of the country. Secondly, Njoya's motivations for political participation are underpinned by a theology of humanity. Njoya views human beings as created in the image of God and thus vested with dignity. Because of this image of God inherent in them, human beings are vested with "sovereignty," which here I read as agency—that is a right to speak, think, and act in a unique manner, and in line with God's ideals for a fully restored life. Third, Njoya's political theology is conscious of political actors who seek to threaten this human sovereignty, revealing that Christian discipleship is a negotiation with political powers that seek to rob people of life.

What emerges from the theological perspective of Njoya is what some scholars have termed "decolonization." This is a critical approach towards the colonial paradigm, an approach that prioritizes epistemologies, voices, and contexts of the colonized, rather than borrowing uncritically from the Western intellectual and historical tradition.[53] Sakupapa, for example, views decolonization as the task of unlinking from the colonial matrix of controlling the economy, knowledge, and authority of a particular people.[54] He observes that theologians such as Kwame Bediako, J. N. K. Mugambi, and Mercy Amba Oduyoye engaged in theological reflection that tried to make sense of their postcolonial orientation, given the history of colonialism that Africa came out of—although he thinks that they did not go far enough in unraveling "the continuity of colonialism." In Africa, this decolonial orientation has been championed in the works of the Senegalese intellectual Cheikh Anta Diop, the Kenyan literary scholar Ngugi wa Thiong'o, and the South African theologian Steve Biko.[55] Within the contemporary context, Naidoo has called for decolonization in South African theological education and Weber has called for decolonization of youth ministry models.[56] Thus, African theology, as exemplified through the political theology of Njoya, has arisen as "decolonial episteme" that takes seriously the struggles,

---

52. Ndereba, "Kenyan Political Theology."
53. Kaunda, "Denial of African Agency," 76; Ward, *Introducing Practical Theology*.
54. Sakupapa, "Decolonising Content," 416, 420.
55. Sakupapa, "Decolonising Content," 417.
56. Naidoo, "Overcoming Alienation"; Weber, "Decolonising Youth Ministry."

sources, and significance of African people and perspectives.[57] The decolonial approach does not seek to downplay the universal—here, I view the universal as that which we can borrow from the Christian tradition in the church in history—but also pays close and critical attention to the particular.[58] For the purposes of this chapter, how the theological methodologies and models we have inherited from the West when it comes to youth ministry approaches must be examined through considering issues that are pertinent in the Kenyan context—political youth agency.

IMPLICATIONS FOR HOLISTIC DISCIPLESHIP

The central thesis of this chapter is that the discipleship model that we are using in Kenyan youth ministry is one that merely focuses on the "spiritual" aspect of Christian life, without the attendant "materiality" that grounds it in everyday lived realities. More specifically, this chapter has explored how these inherited Western models, if uncritically investigated, do not help young people to make sense of and to respond to the political contexts that shape their lives, either positively or negatively. This chapter has made use of Bonhoeffer and Njoya to reveal how the Christian tradition has a universal appeal that must be applied to different contexts—for Bonhoeffer, youth discipleship within Nazi-occupied Germany and for Njoya in Kenya, political engagement within oppressive political regimes. This chapter has also briefly engaged the decolonial discourse, borrowing from its emphasis on theological reflection that foregrounds African voices—in this case Njoya—and one that focuses on struggles in African societies—in this case, how churches can disciple young Kenyans to participate in the political processes of the day. In the following paragraphs, I focus on some implications for various aspects of discipleship in ecclesial spaces.

Expanding the "Conversion-Only" Paradigm

The first implication for discipleship is that youth workers must move from a "conversion-only" paradigm that merely focuses on how many "lost souls were won to Christ." This paradigm utilizes an ephemeral approach to salvation, grounded within a capitalistic mindset of winning versus

---

57. Sakupapa, "Decolonising Content," 418.
58. Kaunda, "Denial of African Agency," 77.

losing. The implication is that our approach to young people tends to be a "hit-and-run" approach, which views them as goods within a spiritual market. Rather, I think we need to view discipleship as a process of following Christ. This way, we view the Christian life not only in its entry point but—borrowing from a Reformed view of salvation—we view it as a past reality (election, justification) with present consequences (sanctification) and future expectations (glorification). What this means is that our work with young people is an ongoing process of formation that has impact in everyday lives—for the purposes of this chapter, an impact that shapes how we respond to the political milieu of our time. Such an approach is what is envisioned by Jesus Christ in his question to the Herodians concerning paying taxes to Caesar (Matt 22:15-22). Jesus' approach is a holistic approach that rejects a dichotomous worldview and foregrounds both the responsibility of human beings created in *imago Dei* to honor God with their whole lives, including their political responsibilities to the authorities of their time. This same argument is extended by the apostle Paul in Rom 13. This does not mean that there is no room for subversive responses to oppressive political regimes (for example, Peter's response to the Sadducees in Acts 5:29), but young people cannot afford to be politically passive.

Discipling Youth for Public Engagement

Secondly, this chapter implies that discipleship is not just a privatized response to Jesus Christ, but a public life of transformation and engagement. The task of youth ministry then is certainly introducing young people to Jesus Christ, yet also preparing them with tools to deal with the public issues that the society faces. Aziz views youth ministry as "public practical theology," noting that this type of ministry approach views young people with the capacity to be theologians and to engage in God's work in their worlds.[59] This chapter has focused on how such a discipleship approach must help young people deal with the sociopolitical contexts of their time through political education, voter registration and turnout, preaching concerning the role of Christians in politics, as well as giving youth agency within ecclesial spaces. Unfortunately, youth voices are not usually accorded a seat at the table of the church's life. Could it be that the reason that Kenyan youth, and in particular Kenyan Christian youth, lack political agency is because their important voices within a hierarchical African

59. Aziz, "Public Practical Theology," 5.

communal context have been ignored (if not rejected)? Youth work within the church must therefore equip young people with the sense of agency, or to use Njoya's words, "sovereignty," to take responsibility for their lives. In my own academic work and practical ministry involvement within the contemporary African context, I can mention several issues that come to mind. First, youth ministries must help young people to navigate the faith-science dichotomy, falsely championed as the only mode of interaction within secular-materialist societies. A practical example is how African (Kenyan) Christians tried to make sense of uptake or rejection of COVID-19 vaccines in the wake of the pandemic. Another example is how the faith-science dialogue features in apologetic engagement with the rising cohorts of African atheists.[60] Second, youth ministries must be embedded in a public theology that can help Kenyan youth to grapple with socioeconomic issues of youth unemployment, social enterprise, inadequate healthcare, Gender Based Violence (GBV), and mental health issues, just to name a few. This type of discipleship aims at restoring the agency, divinely given by God, of young people, and views them as partners with God on his mission to heal the world. Political agency is not just an issue for an election season but has ramifications for everyday aspects of life that African (Kenyan) youth find themselves in.

---

60. Ndereba, "Emerging Themes."

8

Understanding Youth Leaving Faith for Science[1]

THE REALITY OF YOUTH leaving the church is an accepted fact in youth ministry studies. While there are different interpretations of the phenomena, it is evident that in emerging adulthood, young people in a search of individuality often question their communities of faith, with some leaving those communities of faith. Most of the empirical research has been done in the North American context, with key surveys from Barna acting as analytical frameworks for scholarly reflections and their contributions in journal articles, theses, and dissertations. In these studies, different ways of conceptualizing young people who have left the church are proposed. For instance, Kinnaman and Hawkins distinguish between nomads, prodigals, and exiles.[2] According to them, nomads still consider themselves Christian, prodigals have abandoned their Christian identity, and exiles still have a Christian identity but "feel stuck" in the faith and popular culture narrative. Much more will be said concerning these markers.

Large scale surveys that have been foundational for studying youth leaving the church are by scholars like David Kinnaman. In their first book, *Unchristian: What a New Generation Really Thinks About Christianity* . . .

---

1. This chapter is derived with permission from Ndereba, "Nonreligious Identity Formation."

2. Kinnaman and Hawkins, *You Lost Me*, 25.

and Why It Matters, Kinnaman and Lyons studied thousands of sixteen- to twenty-nine-year-olds who were "outsiders" of the faith and the voices of hundreds of pastors and church leaders.[3] By contrast, the more recent *You Lost Me* surveys "insiders" of the faith, that is, those who may have disaffiliated from faith communities but still identify as Christian. The study interviewed 22,103 adults and 2,124 teenagers from across the United States.[4] This in itself offers perspective to the conversation because, as some scholars have intimated, youth leaving the church may not necessarily mean youth leaving the Christian faith altogether. Here, a distinction can be made between "disassociation" and "disidentification." Cronshaw presents another study of this phenomena on youth leaving the faith within an Australian context where they make the distinction that disassociation (or disengagement) is a sociological category of young people who stop affiliating with a particular Christian community while retaining their Christian identity, while disidentification (or deidentification) is the total rejection of one's Christian faith or commitment.[5] Their study, *Hemorrhaging Faith*, focused on eighteen- to thirty-four-year-old Australian youth who had a Christian background, and utilized a mixed-methods approach, combining literature review, semi-structured interviews (qualitative), and two online surveys (quantitative) with a total of 2,049 responses.[6] A similar study has been conducted in Finland, which studies the post-confirmation retention rate of youth (fourteen to twenty-five years) in the Evangelical Lutheran Church of Finland over a ten-year period.[7]

Within the African continent, several studies, mostly masters' theses and doctoral dissertations, have explored the same phenomena. I conducted a study among eighty-eight young people in Nairobi who had left the church.[8] Van As has studied the phenomena within the South African context, using focus groups of young people and parents in Vaalpark, which is situated between Sasolburg and Vanderbijlpark in Free State.[9] While not researching the specific phenomena of youth leaving the church, Weber explores various aspects that either hinder or support the faith formation of

3. Kinnaman and Lyons, *Unchristian*, 15.
4. Cronshaw et al., *Hemorrhaging Faith*, 16.
5. Cronshaw et al., *Hemorrhaging Faith*, 18.
6. Cronshaw et al., *Hemorrhaging Faith*, 17.
7. Niemelä, "No Longer Believing," 177.
8. Ndereba, "Youth Worldviews."
9. Van As, "Leaving the Church," 11.

adolescents (fourteen to seventeen years old) in Evangelical Bible Church of Southern Africa (EBCOSA).[10] These studies are merely representative but are written in the background of the theological framework that many young people have been nurtured in. Globally, this theological framework has been termed Moral Therapeutic Deism (MTD), an outcome of the National Study of Youth and Religion (NSYR), and functions as a way of analyzing the dearth of biblical and theological foundations for youth ministry.[11] Within the West, scholars have critiqued the over-emphasis on a narrowly dichotomous view of ethics, the understanding of God as a genie, and a distant God who is not related in the day-to-day lives of young people.[12] Practical theologians, on the other hand, seek to respond to this dichotomy of ivory-tower theological jargon with entertainment-focused youth ministry by offering a balance between theological reflection that is engaged in the actual lives and practices of young people.[13]

These studies therefore seek to offer theological analyses on why young people are either disaffiliating or disidentifying with faith communities. Weber argues that we need to view youth work as a process of faith formation that enables young people to articulate their faith in their own language.[14] Kinnaman observes similar issues between Protestant youth and Roman Catholic youth who question the relevance of Christian doctrine—particularly teachings on sexuality, marriage, and liturgical practices—in light of their postmodern, post-Christian, and secular contexts.[15] Niemelä also notes a parallel between disaffiliation with changing attitudes of community and belonging among Generation Y (or Millennials).[16] She notes that the search for authenticity within an age of individualism leads young people to question institutions particularly when churches as institutions do not promote a redemptive ethos.

Following this frame of thinking, Fazzino notes that young people who leave the church do so on the premise of negotiating hegemonic cultural forces, particularly within various strands of North American evangelical Christianity.[17] Fazzino applies decolonial thought to analyze the emotional

10. Weber, "Faith Formation."
11. Smith and Denton, *Soul Searching*.
12. Dean, *Almost Christian*, 21.
13. Jacober, *Adolescent Journey*, 11; Root and Dean, *Theological Turn*, 17.
14. Weber, "(South) African Voice," 3.
15. Kinnaman, *You Lost Me*, 23–24.
16. Niemelä, "No Longer Believing," 183.
17. Fazzino, "Leaving the Church."

and cognitive processes involved in young people who leave their faith communities in search of better "paradigms" that can help them deal with social and cultural contradictions.[18] Barreto and Py present the research in the Brazilian context and reveal that those who have left their evangelical identities—what in the literature is "ex-vangelical" or "post-evangelical"—do so on the basis of the ineptitude of "white evangelism" to deal with issues of minority identities.[19] A sociological analysis of this phenomenon is proposed by Glass, Sutton, and Fitzgerald who observe that young people switch between religious traditions in a bid to deal with their process of individuation so as to ensure better outcomes—or outcomes that cohere with their faith perspective—in life in the areas of education, marriage, and other adulthood transitions.[20] Lastly, a major reason given in the literature is that faith communities are ill-equipped in helping young people to integrate their faith with scientific discourse.

VOICES OF KENYAN YOUTH

This chapter therefore seeks to foreground this faith-science dialectic and how it contributes to young people leaving the church. It presents research conducted in 2022 among twenty Kenyan youth who identify as "non-religious" and utilizes a practical theological framework of analysis. While Shantelle Weber and Brandon Weber have offered an analysis of faith and science and youth ministry, what this chapter offers is an empirical methodology that is grounded in a narrative analysis of de-churched youth.[21] The timing could not be more significant with the first photographs of outer space received from the most recent and most advanced telescope in human history, the James Webb telescope. This chapter explores why the faith-science dialogue is so critical for work with young people and will explore several areas of application for faith formational practices among young people in Africa.

Table 1 below represents the target population of the research study. The research instrument was distributed through key youth networks in Nairobi, including the Atheists in Kenya Society, the Free-Thinkers Society in Kenya, Nairobi Youth Workers Network, and the Youth Workers

18. Fazzino, "Leaving the Church," 261.
19. Barreto and Py, "Ex- and Post-Evangelicalism."
20. Glass et al., "Leaving the Faith."
21. Weber and Weber, "'In the Beginning.'"

Network of the PCEA. The research instrument was in the form of an online Google form that was live from March 14, 2022, until April 23, 2022. The instrument was made up of both closed questions, such as on general demographics of age and gender, and open-ended questions for the specific questions surrounding the theme of study. The instrument also utilized Likert scales for key questions—for example, on the compatibilism between faith and science—where:

> One—Strongly Incompatible
> Two—Soft Incompatible
> Three—Neutral
> Four—Soft Compatible
> Five—Strongly Compatible

The instrument received twenty-two responses but was reduced to twenty with two responses being beyond the scope of the research in terms of age (respondent fifteen was forty-four years old and respondent twenty-two was forty years old). Table 1 below represents a summary of the findings.

THE CONCEPT OF NON-RELIGION

Religious studies within the African continent pursue this direction premised on the influential philosopher of religion John Mbiti, who foregrounded the study of religions in Africa through a study of 300 concepts of God on the continent.[22] The statistics within SSA support this thesis that Africa is a highly religious continent. In Kenya's 2019 census, for example, Christianity accounts for 85.5 percent, Islam accounts for 11 percent, while other religious minorities comprise less than 2 percent, including Hindus, Sikhs, Baha'is, and those adhering to various traditional religious beliefs. According to the census, atheists account for 755,750 people in the country, with the three highest atheist counties as Kilifi (146,669), Nakuru (67,640), and Nairobi (54,841). In the census, 73,253 claimed they do not know their religion and 6,909 did not state any religious affiliation.[23] These "neutral" religious identities can be attributed to social stigma particularly significant in a culture that values communalism and rewards in-group notions of trust and togetherness,[24] so the numbers may be higher than those reported.

---

22. Mbiti, *Concepts of God*; Mbiti, *African Religions and Philosophy*.
23. Kenya National Bureau of Statistics, "2019 Kenya Population," 422.
24. Abbott and Mollen, "Atheism"; Devellennes and Loveless, "Tolerance," 5.

Understanding Youth Leaving Faith for Science

Respondent	Age	Town/City	Nonreligious identity	Nonreligious group	Nonreligious group contribution	Previous religious affiliation	Age of disaffiliation	Reason	Faith and science compatibility	Nonreligion influencer
IMS	31	Diani-Galu	Atheist	Yes	Exposure to diversity	Conservative Muslim	23	Diverse perspectives (life in UK and Kenya)	Strong incompatible	Social media
KK	30	Nairobi	Agnostic and atheist	Yes	Exposure to diversity	Christian	21	Citing 1 Cor 13:11, "leaving childish ways"	Strong incompatible	Social media
AT	20	Nairobi	Agnostic atheist	Yes	Critical engagement	Explorative Christian—Baptist, Anglican, Catholic	16	Unanswered questions	Soft compatible	Social media
GK	36	Nairobi, Kenya	Atheist	No	No	Strong Anglican	32	Intellectual questions—Africa, evolution, suffering	Strong incompatible	Social media
MA	31	Mombasa	Atheist	Yes	No	Christian	18	Just happened	Neutral	Social media
KK2	35	Thika	Atheist	Yes	Exposure to diversity	Protestant Christian	16	Love of science—influenced by four horsemen	Neutral	Social media

95

Respondent	Age	Town/City	Nonreligious identity	Nonreligious group	Nonreligious group contribution	Previous religious affiliation	Age of disaffiliation	Reason	Faith and science compatibility	Nonreligion influencer
UA	28	Nairobi	Atheist	No	Exposure to diversity	Christian	23	Intellectual questions	Strong incompatible	Social media
LE	25	Nakuru	Atheist	No	No	Catholic	10	Intellectual questions—history, science, critical thinking	Strong incompatible	Book
LK	21	Mururi	Agnostic	No	Not in a nonreligious group—but same sentiment	Christian	18	Intellectual questions—violence, barbaric laws, sacrifices	Strong incompatible	Social media
ZW	35	Nairobi	Atheist	No	Critical engagement	Christian	22	Just happened	Strong incompatible	Book
MWW	35	Mombasa	Atheist	Yes	Exposure to diversity	Staunch Christian	25	Intellectual questions—immorality advocated by the Bible	Strong incompatible	Social media
EN	22	Eldoret	Atheist	Yes	Not in a nonreligious group	Christian family	17	Irrationality	Neutral	Book

Respondent	Age	Town/City	Nonreligious identity	Nonreligious group	Nonreligious group contribution	Previous religious affiliation	Age of disaffiliation	Reason	Faith and science compatibility	Nonreligion influencer
NNN	27	Kakamega	Atheist	No	Critical engagement	Christian (even part of Church staff)	25		Soft incompatible	Social media
K.I	27	Nairobi	Agnostic	Yes	Exposure to diversity—religion helps people cope with crisis	Christian (even studied theology)		Intellectual questions—moral failures, evolutionary theories, a few people going to heaven, many moral ppl going to hell	Strong compatible	Book
MW	27	Murang'a	Atheist	Yes	Not really	Christian (even youth pastor)	22	"Critical thinking"	Strong incompatible	Social media
FD	24	Nairobi	Atheist	Yes	Not really. "Too much arguing over nothing"	Christian Protestant	19	Philosophy and psychology	Strong incompatible	Printed book atheist

Respondent	Age	Town/City	Nonreligious identity	Nonreligious group	Nonreligious group contribution	Previous religious affiliation	Age of disaffiliation	Reason	Faith and science compatibility	Nonreligion influencer
MM	24	Juja	Humanist	No	No	Christian	20	Analyzing own beliefs	Soft incompatible	Printed books (scientists and atheists)
RM	24	Nairobi	Agnostic	Yes	Exposure to diversity	Christian	8	Hypocrisy	Neutral	Social/digital media
WJ	28	Mbale	Agnostic	Yes	Critical engagement	Christian (SDA)	23	Logical thinking	Strong incompatible	Digital media
JK	21	Nairobi	Atheist	No	Critical engagement	Christian (Roman Catholic)	16	Intellectual issues—Bible's vagueness, proof for God's existence, age of the universe compared to scientific evidence	Strong incompatible	Printed books "I don't rely on internet"

Table 1: *Summary of Findings from Youth Survey on Non-Religion*
(N =twenty; Age m = 27.6 years old; Atheist n = thirteen; Agnostic n = four; Agnostic-atheist n = two; Humanist n = one)

Nonreligion has gained prominence as a sociological category within the West in the past half century.[25] Several institutes and networks, such as the Institute for the Study of Secularism in Society and Culture (ISSSC, founded in 2005) and the International Nonreligion and Secularity Research Network (NSRN, founded in 2008), are markers of empirical approaches to the study of nonreligion.[26] This increased focus can be attributed to the secularization theory suggested in the sociology of religion, following along with rising liberal democracies, modernization, individualism, and free-thinking movements in the West, and originating from the "anthropocentric focus" of the seventeenth- and eighteenth-century enlightenment.[27] Additionally, the growing category of those who are identified as "nones" has piqued the interest of sociologists of religion. However, Berger has revisited his earlier secularization thesis by critically examining the theory, given the growing religiosity in many societies.[28] Gorski and Altınordu argue that what is needed is more empirical approaches that study specific cohorts of the population rather than generalized theories.[29] The rise of religion, and particularly Christianity in the Southern Hemisphere, continues to support this "desecularization" thesis.[30]

Together with the rise of humanist, atheist, and nonreligious groups, markers such as church attendance, religious beliefs, as well as waning religious identities reveal that much of Europe and North America is in a post-Christian context.[31] In the literature, the concept of nonreligion is correlated with either lack of beliefs or lack of affiliation.[32] However, other scholars are more critical toward this approach of objective definition, critiquing it on its overdependence on the concept of "religion," which can be subjective and "fuzzy."[33] For instance, Jong considers a level of "Christian atheism" among liberal Anglicans and "atheistic religiosity" among secular humanists as examples of how boundaries of religion and nonreligion

---

25. Lee, *Recognizing the Non-Religious*; Zuckerman et al., *Nonreligious*, 4.
26. Lee, *Recognizing the Non-Religious*, 4.
27. Taylor, *Secular Age*; Molteni, *Need for Religion*, 10, 221.
28. Berger, *Desecularization of the World*, 2.
29. Gorski and Altınordu, "After secularization?"
30. Jenkins, *Next Christendom*.
31. Zuckerman et al., *Nonreligious*, 5.
32. Clarke, *Oxford Handbook*; Jong, "(Not) Defining (Non)Religion."
33. Jong, "(Not) Defining (Non)Religion."

often oscillate.³⁴ Recent studies on the beliefs and lived realities of atheist scientists unpack how these identities are often nuanced compared to the traditional definitions.³⁵

For instance, Ecklund's and Johnson's research among atheist scientists reveals that some of them value the role of religion in public life or appreciate the role of religion among their religious spouses.³⁶ In the Indian context, Thomas uses ethnographic data from Indian scientists who are identified as atheists and argues that they eschew the simplistic Western labels.³⁷ To him, these biologists, theoretical physicists, ecologists, a scientist in molecular reproduction, and a geometric scientist, while having strong Darwinist and materialist influences, categorize themselves as "agnostics," "sceptics," and "nontheists."³⁸ More instructively, Thomas proposes that where these Indian strands of atheisms differs from the Western counterparts is how they still value traditional religious ideas, practices, and symbols—for example, religious naming, festivals, songs, and pilgrimages.³⁹

Additionally, Lee, collating research in the field of nonreligion, observes how atheism could be defined as "hard" or "soft," "positive" or "negative," and secularism can be understood as "moderate" or "radical."⁴⁰ Lee's contribution is that she creates a theoretical framework for substantive definitions and understandings of what nonreligion is rather than what it is not. These pointers in the literature reveal broader definitions of the concepts beyond the usual popular representations of the same in society. This chapter seeks to go beneath the popular presentations of faith and science among nonreligious youth by considering the actual data from African nonreligious youth.

---

34. Jong, "(Not) Defining (Non)Religion," 21.

35. Elsdon-Baker, "Hardline 'Secular' Evolutionists"; Ecklund and Johnson, *Atheism in Science*.

36. Ecklund and Johnson, *Atheism in Science*.

37. Thomas, "Unbelief Among Indian Scientists," 46.

38. Thomas, "Unbelief Among Indian Scientists," 56.

39. Thomas, "Unbelief Among Indian Scientists," 59–60.

40. Lee, *Recognizing the Non-Religious*, 8.

A NEGLECTED AREA OF STUDY: NONRELIGION IN AFRICA

Despite the fact that religion is still central to African societies, an interesting demographic needs critical investigation. With the rise of atheist and humanist societies in parts of Africa like Cape Town, Johannesburg, Lagos, Nairobi, and Accra, sociological studies that foreground this African phenomenon are needed. This chapter explores African nonreligious youth in Kenya through a qualitative study in order to investigate the science and faith dialogue that is central in the field of study. Although religious studies in the continent reveal a significant body of work from sociological, theological, philosophical, and psychological perspectives, there is a gap in scholarly attention on nonreligion in the continent. This chapter seeks to contribute to the research on the relationship between science and belief in the Global South, particularly from a Kenyan context.

Nonreligion is defined from the locus of religion. Within sociological research, religious identity is examined in its relationship with families of origin or experiences with institutionalized forms of religion.[41] However, both nonreligious and religious identity are growing in complexities given more individualistic approaches to religion and spirituality, access to plurality in worldview options as a result of digital cross-pollination, and the growth of scientific development that has led to more critical approaches towards inherited traditions and cultures. This has led to broadened definitions of terms such as "religious" or "nonreligious."[42] Much more research is needed within the SSA context, so as to contribute meaningfully to the rich conversation within the global context.

KENYAN NON-RELIGIOUS YOUTH: VIEWS OF FAITH AND SCIENCE

Examining the intersection between youth and nonreligion, some scholars have painted a broad brush on the canvas that reveals three related areas: society/institutions, personal experiences, and gender/sexuality.[43] Both from literature and anecdotal experiences, there has been a growing dissatisfaction between young people and institutions such as schools,

---

41. Spickard, *Alternative Sociologies of Religion*, 14.
42. Cotter, *Critical Study of Non-Religion*.
43. Arweck and Shipley, *Young People*.

universities, governments, and churches. Part of this growing divide can be attributed to the collapse of institutions and their failure to assist young people to successfully transition into adulthood.

Young people's personal experiences with those who are different than them in the context of increasingly plural societies means that they have a wider appreciation of other people's beliefs and identities than prior generations. This is as true in more culturally liberal Western societies as it is within more conservative African societies. Writing for the British context, Madge, Hemming, and Stenson investigate how rural urban migrations affect young people's engagement with religion especially as a result of increasing liberal values and conflicting discourses on individual rights.[44] Within the context of gender and sexuality, the rise of gender minorities within African contexts has been received in mixed ways.

All this means that the concept of identity is more fluid and possibly fragmented, as compared to decades prior where communities were more monolithic. Within the Kenyan context, a research study explores the worldview construction among eighty-eight "de-churched" youth in Nairobi.[45] What emerged within the study supports the wider academic studies surrounding those who have left "organized Christianity." Reasons for these nonreligious identities could be traced to factors such as divergent philosophical views concerning reality, broadened religious identities, moral failures of religious leaders, the rise of scientism and its combative posture toward religions, and the absence of "open spaces" that would allow young people to safely critique their own perspectives. Given the massive shifts within post-COVID contexts, the number of young people being disillusioned with religious institutions has been growing in light of recent narratives of religious "deconstruction."[46]

Within Christian studies, these deconstructed religious identities have critiqued notions of institutions, faith, and identity with the goal of spearheading more innovative, individualistic, and affirming expressions of Christianity.[47] The research instrument was designed using Google Forms with the aim of collecting data around specific thematic areas. The method utilized a questionnaire since the research was conducted during the

---

44. Madge et al., *Youth on Religion*, 2.
45. Ndereba, "Youth Worldviews."
46. Mudge, "What Is Faith Deconstruction?"
47. Marti and Ganiel, *Deconstructed Church*.

COVID-19 pandemic, which made face-to-face, focused group interviews, for example, slightly difficult.

The questionnaire included a number of open-ended questions that allowed for respondents to articulate their "context-specific" views.[48] Given that the research is focused on young people, age was a critical consideration. Appreciating how complex nonreligious identities can be viewed in the Kenyan context, open-ended questions were used, which allowed the respondents to define their nonreligious identity using their own words. The research also incorporated a question that explored the role of nonreligious groups or societies in their nonreligious identity formation, and these are discussed in the following sections. The role of nonreligious authority figures in youth nonreligious identity formation was explored, particularly through either their authoritative texts or social media presence. The research instrument also tested the level of compatibility or incompatibility between faith and science and their impact on nonreligious identities as well as their role in answering the big questions of life. The research instrument went live on March 14, 2022, and remained live until April 23, 2022. The research instrument was piloted to ensure it fits in with the scope of the International Research Network for the Study of Science and Belief in Society (INSSBS). Given the minority status of nonreligious youth in Kenya, the research instrument was distributed digitally through youth networks, that is, Apologetics Kenya, Nairobi Youth Workers Network, Atheists in Kenya, and Kenyan Free Thinkers groups.

Further, this research was based on a purposive nonprobability sampling method.[49] The research instrument was initially distributed on March 14, 2022, and got eleven responses. It was resubmitted on April 20, 2022, to seek more female respondents. The total responses came to twenty-two. The only female response was from a forty-four-year-old lady; she was excluded from the analysis due to her age demographic not fitting the research target of "youth." This brought the total analyzed responses to twenty since one other response was ignored due to age limit, that is, forty years old. Twenty responses were seen as sufficient in ensuring against research saturation.[50] The responses based on the various questions in the research instrument are captured in Table 1.

---

48. Marvasti, *Qualitative Research in Sociology*, 12.
49. Merriam and Tisdell, *Qualitative Research*, 96.
50. Merriam and Tisdell, *Qualitative Research*, 101.

Nonreligious Identity

Although nonreligious identities are many, most participants in this chapter are identified as atheist (n = 13); four are identified as agnostic (n = 4) and two as "atheist and agnostic" (n = 2); one is identified as humanist (n = 1). While providing the nonreligious identity options "atheist," "agnostic," or "other," the research instrument included an open-ended section to allow for more variation in nonreligious identification. However, it seems that for the participants, nonreligious identities occur primarily across agnostic and atheistic identities, with a small minority being humanist. This could be as a result of the salience of organized nonreligion or restricted latitude in the participant's nonreligious understanding. Further studies could unpack these nonreligious identifications to study whether there is any ambivalence in nonreligious identification in the Kenyan context, similar to what Lee has argued for within a North American context.[51]

Nonreligious Groups

Most participants see a positive role of nonreligious groupings to their nonreligious identities. From the researcher's coding of the data, two contributions of nonreligious groups emerged, namely, exposure and critical engagement. It seems that for most participants, their core concern in religion or nonreligion was dealing with diversity of views or ability to critically engage with this diversity. For instance, statements from two participants are as follows:

> Due to free exchange of ideas among members, better understanding of the world is bound. (KK)

> It has exposed me to debate and different perspectives. (IMS)

These positive contributions of nonreligious groups to nonreligious identity formation can be interpreted in the reasons for disaffiliation. Most respondents view their previous religious affiliations as unhelpful to their intellectual questions, view Christian representations of suffering as problematic, and see Christian complicity with injustices in contemporary religious life, among many other issues. Additionally, some viewed religion as a static body of beliefs that are resistant to change, whereas science allowed for them to examine facts and change positions with better evidence.

---

51. Lee, "Ambivalent Atheist Identities."

Nonreligious groups were therefore seen as helping the respondents to examine beliefs about the world that they had been exposed to in their earlier years, as well as to cognitively resolve their intellectually problematic issues.

Previous Religious Affiliation

Most respondents came from a religious background. This can be correlated to the religiosity that is part of Kenyan societal life. Christianity (85.5 percent) and Islam (11 percent) contribute significant percentages of the religious affiliation of Kenyans. In the 2019 Kenyan census, Protestants, Roman Catholics, and Evangelical churches accounted for 33.4 percent, 20.6 percent, and 20.4 percent, respectively, among the Christian population.[52] Among the twenty research participants, nineteen came from a Christian background while one came from a Muslim background.

Among the Christians, some used particular markers such as "staunch," "strong," "born again," "baptized," and "saved" to describe how deeply involved they were in their Christian upbringing. Others also noted "raised in a Christian family," revealing how religious affiliation is also transmitted through the family unit. This supports the sociological research that reveals how belief is connected to belonging and how religious belief and unbelief is transmitted through families.[53] Although religious belief may not always be consistently transmitted, the argument is that family background influences how youth engage with religion.

Two responses were coded as "explorative Christian" to show how, as per their responses, these two specific people had gone through two or more Christian identities. For example, AT was formerly identified as Baptist, Anglican, and Catholic. Although these Christian identities (or denominations) may have some strong divergences on particular religious beliefs, young people's "multiple belonging" reveals how ambivalent young people are with regard to specific denominational beliefs.[54] According to the research participants, religion is thus seen as more than merely particular beliefs.

---

52. Kenya National Bureau of Statistics, "2019 Kenya Population," 12.
53. Catto and Eccles, "(Dis)Believing and Belonging," 47.
54. Okwuosa et al., "Double Denominational Belonging."

Reasons for Religious Disaffiliation

Most of the reasons given by the research participants concerning their disaffiliation was the inability of their religious background in helping them to deal with their intellectual questions. It is interesting to correlate the age of disaffiliation among the participants with the developmental stage of emerging adulthood. As a growing research area in developmental psychology, emerging adulthood is seen as a period of extending adolescence beyond the late teens into the mid-twenties.[55] Arnett, a key theorist of emerging adulthood, for example, notes how the identity crisis of emerging adulthood is a reality of young people in this stage of life who are participating in post-secondary education, expressing greater tolerance in premarital sexual activities and cohabitation, and delaying marriage and parenthood.[56] In the Kenyan context, the eighteen- to thirty-year-old bracket is the time of university education, entry into the labor market, and the consequential exposure to and engagement with divergent worldviews. With these significant life changes that happen in the lives of young people, questions of origin, purpose, morality and destiny are common. The research respondents suggested that organized religious communities did not help them answer these important questions.

> I felt like there were many gaps in Christianity, i.e., wondering why Africans don't feature in the Bible yet science (evolution) puts across a very convincing case that Africa is the cradle of mankind. Evolution theory sounds more convincing to me than the Bible's creation theory, which doesn't feature Africans. I wondered how God can love us all equally, then allow people in developing countries to suffer more than the counterparts in developed countries. These concerns prompted me to look for like-minded people online and locally. (GK)

> I struggled with the question of suffering, and I didn't find the Christian answer to it sufficient. I was thinking of going into missions and wanted to know why non-Christians, i.e., Muslims, Hindus, etc. don't believe in the Bible and Christianity. This made me want to understand Christianity better. I took a deep dive into learning about the history of the church and the origin of the Bible using academic lectures available on YouTube. Later, wanting to understand non-Christians, I watched a lot of atheist versus

---

55. Arnett, "Emerging Adulthood."
56. Arnett, "Emerging Adulthood, 70–71.

Christian debates. Trying to understand the issues [like] why they didn't believe. But then I started wrestling with some of the points atheists raised because they were actually valid. This took a period of several months until in 2020, when the COVID-19 pandemic happened, it occurred to me that a loving God wouldn't send viruses to kill millions. And I knew we would only see a scientific solution and not a supernatural solution. Then I embraced skepticism. (NNN)

Evidently, key questions that emerge among nonreligious youth include the colonial history of Kenya (and Africa) and the place of religion, the religious understanding of creation vis-à-vis the scientific theory of evolution, as well as dealing with the problematic issues of religion and religious texts—including contemporary suffering, the reality of violence in the Old Testament, and understanding the ancient contexts and sacrifices that color much of Christian understanding. For the respondents, their leaving of organized religion was premised on the fact that their communities of faith did not help them explore these important questions.

FAITH SCIENCE APPROACHES: CONFLICT VERSUS COMPATIBILISM

The heart of this research is exploring the role of faith and science dialogue in the nonreligious identity formation of Kenyan youth. One of the questions used a Likert scale—one (strongly incompatible) to five (strongly compatible)—to measure the level of compatibility between faith and science among the nonreligious youth. The results were as follows:

- A majority of the respondents view faith and science as "strongly incompatible" (n = thirteen).
- A minority view faith and science as neutral (n = four).
- A minority of views reveal either "soft compatibility" (n = one) or "soft incompatibility" (n = one).
- A minority view faith and science as "strongly compatible" (n = one).

Factors Contributing to Compatibility

Those who view religion and science as compatible have a wider understanding of the role of both religion and science. According to some participants,

> Scientists can be and are religious. However, it occasionally means that they have to ignore their beliefs. (AT)

> In many ways, they are compatible. This is because religion is largely moral in nature, while science is more material. The contrast comes in when religion tries to explain the genesis of the material world, which science refutes. (KI)

One of the respondents with a neutral view on the compatibility of faith and science based their argument on the scientific enterprise as probabilistic:

> Most theories before carried out are not necessarily based on evidence but probabilities of the unknown before being actualized. (RM)

In summary, nonreligious Kenyan youth who think religion and science are compatible base their argument on the following:

- The value of religion in answering some of the big questions, for example, morality
- The distinct natures of religion and science—one respondent, for example, demarcated the religious sphere as dealing with more moral questions, while the scientific experience deals more of the material questions
- The presence of believing scientists—one respondent, however, claimed that such scientists have to jettison their faith as they conduct their scientific enterprises
- The humanitarian progress of religion as valuable, for example, in the growth of schools and hospitals in Kenya's history

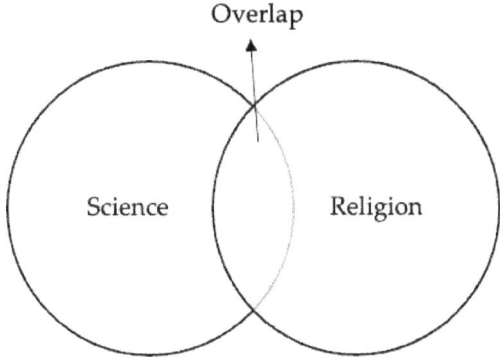

Figure 4: Diagram Showing Science-Religion Overlap

Factors Contributing to Incompatibility

Strong views on incompatibility have to do mainly with the definition and understanding of both faith (for the purpose of this research, "religion") and science. Those who revealed a strong view of incompatibility between religion and science, largely base their understanding of religion as myth and science as fact.

Respondents who viewed religion as incompatible with science based their view largely on the areas of nonoverlap between the two. Most cite evolutionary theory, creation stories, the nature of evidence, historical narratives such as Galileo's arrest, and the incompatibility of faith and reason. These are the common themes in the religion and science debate within contemporary research. Dixon, for example, notes how the history of science reveals that the relationship between religion and science eschews simplistic contemporary views on both sides of the equation.[57]

Dixon helpfully nuances the conflict by noting that the issue is not a generalized view of religion, or of science for that matter, but specific beliefs about a particular religion and specific scientific views.[58] An example is how within both religious and scientific communities, there are divergent views on the theory of evolution. A surprising fact is how Muslim scholars helped to translate Darwin's evolutionary works or the diversity of creationism into old-earth, young-earth, creationist-evolutionist, and intelligent design

---

57. Dixon, *Science and Religion*, 3.
58. Dixon, *Science and Religion*, 4.

(ID) categories.[59] Although science and religion have distinct spheres of operation—for example, science may tell us of the configuration of DNA or the mechanisms of online digital systems, while religion may speak of a heaven or hell or the concept of salvation—real contentions, from the research, arise from the areas of overlap, as can be seen in Figure 1. A case in point is that both science and religion make claims on the origin of the universe that are interpreted differently by different people, even those who share similar religious or nonreligious convictions.

Depending on how people approach these, they can either view religion and science as compatible or incompatible and may in turn either nuance their religious or nonreligious identities. The research also revealed that figures of authority as well as social media (or new media) were contributing factors to the respondents' nonreligious identity formation. One of the questions was designed to test whether the respondents' religious identity was formed largely by one of the following:

- Digital platform of prominent scientist
- Digital platform of prominent atheist
- Printed book on a scientific topic
- Printed book from a nonreligious thinker

"Digital platform of prominent scientist" ranked top, with most responses revealing that their nonreligious identity (atheist, agnostic, agnostic-atheist) has been formed largely through the digital platforms of prominent atheists. The respondents cited YouTube channels of the "Four Horsemen": Richard Dawkins, Christopher Hitchens, Daniel Dennett, and Sam Harris. This supports the research that traces the interconnection of youth nonreligion and atheism, with online cultures within the digitally native generations.[60] This categorization of "atheist" and "scientist" was used in order to understand the influencers of nonreligious youth. Will Mason-Wilkes notes how the responses from nonreligious youth are telling, as it portrays their view that the terms "scientist" and "atheist" are synonymous.[61] This is quite revealing given only really one of the "Four Horsemen"—Dawkins—is a "scientist" (and most of his scientific work he

---

59. Dixon et al., *Science and Religion*, 11; Szerszynski, "Understanding Creationism and Evolution," 156.

60. Catto and Eccles, "(Dis)Believing and Belonging," 53.

61. Email conversation with author on May 20, 2022.

did a long time ago)—Dennett is a philosopher; Hitchens is a journalist/pundit; and Harris is a philosopher who calls himself a neuroscientist. Other responses included the printed books of nonreligious thinkers, with one noting that they embraced atheism before the boom of digital media. Others cited the writings of Yuval Noah, Malcolm Gladwell, Jordan Peterson, and Albert Einstein as contributing to their nonreligious identities.

Religious Views of Nonreligious Youth

Finally, most respondents revealed a hostile perspective toward religion in their responses. Although some noted that they would not debate religious people or that they respect others' religious affiliations even though they make no sense to them, they described religion in the following ways:

- "Derailing critical thinking and undermines scientific progress"
- Hampers personal and societal development
- "It does not change, it is archaic"
- "It encroaches on personal autonomy and freedom"
- "It was brought by colonists and Arab conquests"
- "It is a tool of exploitation of the poor"
- Focused on otherworldliness rather than today's issues
- It is about "chasing blessings, favor, money, and so on, through faith"

Only three responses to the question "Do you think religion is beneficial to the progress of African societies?" seemed sympathetic to religion:

> Social mobilization and humanitarian work, e.g., mission hospitals and schools, help to solve actual problems in society. (NNN)
>
> History teaches us so. (KI)
>
> It instills a sense of hope and purpose in most people and maintains law and order. (MW)

Interestingly, both NNN and MW were pastoral staff in their previous religious communities. However, their responses show how ambivalent the science-religion dialogue is among different groups of people. MW, for example, noted that science and religion are strongly incompatible because "the two disciplines seem to not have the same conclusions." However, while his incompatibility rests on the different functions of both domains, he still appreciates the role of religion in giving hope and maintaining order in the society.

What requires more research is the strong incompatibility of science and religion among nonreligious (atheist) Kenyan youth. Is it due to generalizations informed by their authority figures, or merely personal opinion or biases by their nonreligious group "beliefs?" It would be interesting to bring this incompatibility alongside Mason-Wilke's findings where he contrasts media representations of science as either religious, when it is presented as dogmatic, or secular, when it is presented as provisional.[62] Likewise, popular religion that is presented as oversimplistic fails to supply the explanatory justification needed by young people navigating cultural transformations, digital spaces, as well as complex questions. As some have argued, nonreligious identity can be correlated with strong incompatible views between science and religion, while religious identity can be correlated with compatibility between science and religion, even though particular views on each may differ from person to person depending on the specific "content" of either domain of knowledge.[63]

TOWARDS INTEGRATING FAITH AND SCIENCE IN YOUTH MINISTRY

This chapter provides a social science perspective on the faith-science dialogue within the particular context of nonreligious Kenyan youth. The research revealed that while Kenya is considered as a religious nation, there is a growing demographic of those who are identified as nonreligious. Although nonreligious is an identity marker that can be simplistically understood as a sociological category, this research confirmed studies that show that nonreligion can be ambivalent, and this is seen among Kenyan youth who are identified as both agnostic and atheist as well as atheist youth who reveal that their unbelief has not been fostered within a nonreligious group setting.

This chapter revealed several insights. First, nonreligious identification is common across the period of emerging adulthood. The research shows how youth social groups with young people in their late teens and twenties can provide them with spaces to wrestle with the intellectual questions raised by religious faiths. Some of the challenges within the Kenyan

---

62. Mason-Wilkes, "Divine DNA," 22.
63. Leicht et al., "Content Matters," 5.

context, as per the research respondents, include theodicies (i.e., theistic arguments dealing with the problem of pain, evil, and suffering), the missionary and colonial historical past and its antecedents today, the problems posed by a type of Christianity that promises material prosperity but leaves those affiliating with these types of Christian expressions poor, and the difficulties of Biblical interpretation—including the problem of violence in the Old Testament, the cultural distance between the contemporary reader and the ancient Near Eastern context of rites such as sacrifices and other rituals, and the reality of hell as a theological category in Christian thought.

Second, this research reveals that the science and religion dialogue is critical to have so as to create deeper understanding within religious and nonreligious communities. Religious communities could benefit through providing spaces where young people exposed to scientific thought can wrestle with specific religious claims, such as the religious teaching on creation. I have explored how such spaces of exploration can be implemented in light of the communality ("ubuntu") aspect of African cultures, while viewing the unique developmental challenges of young people in a holistic manner that bridges their affective and cognitive aspects.[64] Nonreligious communities could benefit through moving beyond the usual caricature of strong incompatibility that is part of popular atheist literature. Through foregrounding the faith and science dialogue, both groups would appreciate the nuanced understanding in history and contemporary practice, both within and across their different groups.

More importantly, this study contributes to the study of faith and science, particularly among young, nonreligious Kenyans. Much of the literature remains largely Western, and this chapter adds a critical voice from the African context and particularly an East African and Kenyan perspective. This enriches the international scope of the work that INSSBS seeks to do and provides room for further research. Possible future research could explore more specific thematic areas, for instance, concerning specific scientific elements such as evolutionary theory. Further research could also target religious youth in Kenya or across Africa, thereby widening the scope and also providing room for comparative research. Further studies could also pursue a longitudinal approach to test whether the perspectives of faith and science among nonreligious Kenyan youth change over time or are static. This study is merely a surface of an iceberg, yet one that reveals the undercurrents within contemporary studies of religion and science as well as youth religion and nonreligion.

64. Ndereba, "Ubuntu Apologetics."

9

Raising Youth Ecotheologians

CLIMATE CHANGE AND ENVIRONMENTAL degradation are issues that move beyond intellectual discourse and touch the everyday lived realities of people across the world. Climate change issues include temperature and rainfall variability, loss of biodiversity, and ocean acidification, among others.[1] In Kenya particularly, the recent drought presents an acute indicator of the scale of drastic changes that the environment presents to the habitability of humanity in all corners of the globe but also to the social, economic, geographical, and agricultural aspects so central to human life. The National Drought Management Authority (NDMA) is a public body established by the NDMA Act 2016, to develop policy and build participatory action in drought management so as to safeguard the country's Vision 2030 for Arid and Semi-Arid Lands (ASALs).[2] While other countries suffer drought, such environmental challenges affect less developed and marginalized areas in profound ways.[3] For instance, not only does drought significantly affect the natural environment, but it also impacts issues as diverse as food security and economic mobility. The UN has proposed an intervention of raising

---

1. Conradie, "Tasks of Christian Ecotheology," 4; Nyerere et al., "Kenya's Climate Change Policy," 5.

2. Government of Kenya, "Vision 2030 Development Strategy," 113.

3. Deane-Drummond, *Primer in Ecotheology*, 1; Miano, "Press Statement on Drought."

$472.6 million to help 4.3 million drought-affected people in 2023.[4] ASALs of Kenya are on a downward spiral in terms of access to water and sanitation, with ripple effects on young people's education that lead to spiraling dropout rates. In terms of the policy environment, Kenya operates under the guidelines of the following documents: the National Climate Change Action Plan 2018–2022 (NCCAP), the National Climate Change Policy 2018, and the Climate Change Act 2016.[5] Climate change is comprehensive in its adverse effects on human populations.

Various youth actors have responded to these climate crises in different ways. The Faith for Earth Youth Council of the UN brings together young faith leaders across various faith traditions and backgrounds to champion informed responses to the climate crisis. The Green Anglicans movement of Kenya, founded in 2018, is another visible response from the church in Kenya that has engaged in various initiatives and activities of climate justice. It covers ten dioceses in the Anglican province of Kenya. Within the discourse on climate change, "climate justice" is emerging as a call to action with the aim of ensuring sustainable and equitable futures for the world's vulnerable. These approaches to the climate crisis take on various religious and political angles.

Religious approaches are usually anchored in theological perspectives on humanity or the place of the environment. The more religiously affirmative approaches consider the world as a created habitat for the well-being of humanity. According to Chitando, religious critics argue that Christianity, with its close ties to empire and capitalism, views the earth as an unlimited resource to be maximally depleted for human development.[6] What may be said is that approaches to the environment cannot be oversimplified. By "mapping environmental theology," this chapter unearths the ways that young people, themselves marginalized in these conversations, envisage the thematic connections between Christianity and the environment. While environmental theologies have taken more systematic and philosophical approaches to the climate crisis, this chapter grounds the discussion within an empirical framework that centers the voices of young Presbyterians in this important dialogue. The reasons are as follows.

First, young people comprise a significant majority of most of African societies. However, their voices are usually "hashed" due to supposed

---

4. United Nations, "United Nations and Partners."
5. Apollo, "Challenges and Opportunities," 5.
6. Chitando, "Introduction: African Perspectives," 4.

identity cataclysms as well as minimalized agency, informed by harsh cultural underpinnings. Second, this chapter argues that youth agency is critical, not only for climate justice but also for the impact of African Christianity and theology within the continent. World Christianity, a growing enterprise in Christian missions as transnational and transcontinental, must also be transgenerational—meaning that World Christianity should pay attention to how the world's largest population is engaging with important issues in Christian mission, Christian theology, and Christian public engagement. Third, this chapter is methodologically helpful because it furthers the cause of epistemologies and theologies from below, which pay close attention to lived realities and listen to God's voice as he speaks and acts through his people—his young people. By utilizing an empirical approach, this chapter allows for theology to be both attentive and critical to a multiplicity of contexts.

ECOTHEOLOGY: HISTORY, APPROACHES, AND CONTEMPORARY FORMULATIONS

Environmental theology has received significant attention from various scholars. Conradie has argued that ecological theology is a contextual theology that seeks to respond to environmental degradation and injustices.[7] He also expands the theological approach as one that retrieves the Christian tradition and its significance for the climate crisis of our time. I have also pursued a similar line by observing how environmental theology has developed as a theology of context, much like liberation theology emerged within the African American racial context, and how it fills a significant gap in African Christianity and theologizing.[8] These African approaches, in addition to many more, hone in on the African continent by building up on the work of other Christian scholars of the environment like Teilhard de Chardin and Lynne White. More recently, climate justice has emerged as a concept that attends to the mutuality required in Global North and Global South partnerships for climate change mitigation and adaptation strategies in terms of "global solidarity and investment of diverse resources."[9]

The historical development of the field of ecotheology is also discernible. Conradie notes that beginning in the 1970s and focusing on the

---

7. Conradie, *Christianity and Ecological Theology*.
8. Ndereba, "Environmental Justice and Ecumenism."
9. Chitando, "Introduction: African Perspectives," 1.

relationship between humanity and the environment, in the context of environmental ethics, ecotheology has broadened its scope to considering geographical and confessional approaches (e.g., Global North versus Global South), exploring creation in light of the doctrine of God in Abrahamic religions and indigenous religions, as well as intersectional perspectives to the discourse along gender, racial, and ethnic lines.[10] An example of a gender perspective to ecotheology is the rise of ecofeminism, which centers women's voices, reflections, and actions in the crushing realities of the ecological crisis, thereby deconstructing androcentric and patriarchal norms that sideline the agency of women, especially in the context of climate change.[11] The regional perspectives retrieve the richness and relevance of indigenous epistemologies for theological reflection of the environment, especially within the Global South context. Deane-Drummond observes a similar trajectory in the growth of ecotheology from an anthropocentric focus to a biocentric focus (a focus on biological organisms), and finally, a theocentric focus.[12]

These approaches tend to be multi-disciplinary in nature, making use of philosophical, social scientific, economic, cultural, and historical perspectives in the elucidation of ecological issues. While this shows that ecotheology has developed as a field of study, it seems that the discussions have remained within the halls of academia and within the boundaries of conferences. These ecotheologies have not trickled down to the churches and especially to young people. When asked for biblical guidelines around how to engage with the environment, young people did not have much to say. There is need to first and foremost develop a biblical theology of the environment. What might this look like?

God has created a fruitful world full of peace and security and habitable for the holistic flourishing of human and created life. The reality of sin, however, introduces not only human-centered issues such as greed but also cosmological crises that affect the habitable environment. Thorns and thistles now reflect how the fruitful, created world now suffers ecological crises. The rest of the Old Testament contains vistas of a new, created world where humans will live again in shalom with God and the created world (See, for example, Isiah's vision of the new heavens and the new earth in Isa 11). Romans 8 expands the doctrine of salvation, saving it from a gnostic

10. Conradie, "Tasks of Christian Ecotheology," 2.
11. Orevillo-Montenegro, "Eco-Feminism and Eco-Feminist Theology," 235.
12. Deane-Drummond, *Primer in Ecotheology*, 11.

reading that devalues the embodied and enfleshed reality by noting the cosmic ramifications of salvation. The earth groans for the revelation of the sons of God, showing that the earth, too, participates in the redemption of God. This finds climax in the apocalyptic revelation of John who describes the new heavens and new earth in heavenly language that transcends our human imagination. In view of this, while Christians focus on a "spiritual reality" of heaven, they live out their Christian life within a "physical reality." If there is an over-emphasis of heaven without appropriate care of the earth now, then we may resort to an inhumane environment that is harsh and that crushes the lives of people, thereby hindering God's desire for shalom.

YOUTH ECOTHEOLOGICAL AGENCY IN SELECT AFRICAN SCHOLARSHIP

In light of the emphasis of this research, the *HTS Theological Studies* journal had a special issue in 2021 on "Youth, Faith, Climate Change, and Environmental Consciousness: A Case for Sustainable Development." The special issue takes a multidisciplinary perspective on the environment. For instance, Baron interprets environmental theology as a missiological strategy in view of black consciousness, Weber and Weber analyze environmental theology within the broader discourse of faith and science, Beukes outlines the various ways in which young people are taking responsibility when it comes to the climate justice issues, and Aziz studies the intersection of the environment and young people in the Cape Flats area.[13] While both Aziz and Beukes tackle youth agency within their specific contexts, their approaches are largely abstract yet important arguments that center the voices of young people, especially those who are negatively and unequally affected by climate injustice. The gap they leave unaddressed is in what ways and how exactly young people, from their actual voices, can participate in the dialogue. Within the Kenyan context, Maseno and Mamati focus their research among Pentecostal youth.[14] This is laudable, given the fact that the Pentecostal stream of Christianity presents a significant bloc of African Christianity. Elsewhere, Mamati and Maseno also unpack the interface of African traditional religious worldview among the Sengwer and its

---

13. Baron, "Protecting Our Environment"; Weber and Weber, "'In the Beginning'"; Aziz, "Environmental Justice"; Beukes, "Environmental Consciousness."

14. Maseno and King'asia, "Pentecostal Eco-Theology."

negotiation with the environmental issues facing this community.[15] Other scholars have noted how environmental theology has been integrated in the curriculum of various African institutions so as to safeguard sustainable development[16] This chapter adds to these voices, by studying Kenyan Presbyterian Christianity among young people grounded in lived theology as the research paradigm.

THE ECCLESIOLOGICAL CONTEXT: THE PRESBYTERIAN CHURCH OF EAST AFRICA

The ecclesiological context of the study is the PCEA. Maseno notes the central place that Ludwig Krapf has played in the modern missionary expansion in Africa through the Anglican Church Missionary Society (ACMS).[17] Together with his wife, he arrived in Zanzibar in 1844 and later moved to Mombasa. Together with his colleague Rebmann, they were involved in translating the New Testament into Nyika, Kiswahili, and other languages.[18] Scottish Missionaries were antecedent to Presbyterianism in the continent. In the 1880s they set foot in East Africa. Duncan observes that they were instrumental in the formation of the Presbyterian Church of South Africa (PCSA) in 1897.[19]

Muita traces the routes of the PCEA to the Imperial British East Africa Chartered Company (IBEA) incorporated in 1888 for the purposes of trade.[20] William MacKinnon, a member of IBEA, was also a member of the Free Church of Scotland, which had broken off from the established Church of Scotland in 1843. Concerned for the spiritual welfare of the people under their jurisdiction, William MacKinnon and Alexander Bruce formed the East African Scottish Mission in 1889, and upon a formal request by the two, the Rev. James Stewart DD of Lovedale, South Africa, took charge of the work, traveling northwards to Kenya in 1891.[21] Mission stations would be established in Kibwezi on October 15, 1891; in Kikuyu in 1900; by teacher and evangelist Petro Mugo in Tumutumu in 1908; in

15. Mamati and Maseno, "Environmental Consciousness."
16. Chabata, "Sustainable Development in Zimbabwe."
17. Maseno, "Christianity in East Africa," 110.
18. Maseno, "Christianity in East Africa," 110.
19. Duncan, "Politics of Credentials," 306.
20. Muita, *Hewn from the Quarry*, 1.
21. Muita, *Hewn from the Quarry*, 2; PCEA, *Practice and Procedure*, 1.

Chogoria in 1915; and finally the Kambui mission was established under the Gospel Missionary Society in 1945.

Muita has divided the PCEA historical periods instructively. Lighting the torch through the oversees mission efforts between 1891 and 1920, a time of PCEA taking responsibility from the oversees missionaries between 1920 and 1945, social reconstruction after World War II and Africanizing the church between 1945 and 1956, church autonomy between 1956 and 1968, new mission emphases between 1968 and 1991, and the articulation of a new vision into the new millennium.[22] Of special mention is the year 1956, when the Church of Scotland Oversees Presbytery of Kenya and the Synod of the Presbyterian Church of East Africa united through a scheme of union and inaugurated its first General Assembly on February 11, 1956, at St. Andrew's Church, Nairobi.[23] Rev. Robert MacPherson was the first moderator of the General Assembly, serving two terms. In addition, PCEA's contribution to the African church is the Jitegemea philosophy that pushed for self-autonomy based on the Very Rev. Dr. John Gatu's moratorium on foreign assistance in 1971. This has been noted by several historians including Hastings and Muita.[24] This philosophy had the undercurrents of the national motto of Harambee ("Let's all pull together"). Under Rev. MacPherson's leadership, a new emphasis in youth work would begin, which has since shaped the understanding and implementation of youth work in the country.

LISTENING TO THE VOICES OF ENVIRONMENTALLY-CONSCIOUS, YOUNG PRESBYTERIANS

This research is situated within the field of practical theology, which is to say, theology that takes one's context seriously while expanding its interdisciplinary scope. This research pursues this approach by engaging environmental theology with a qualitative study of young people's views on the environment. More specifically, this chapter assumes a "lived theology" approach, which has emerged as a method of theology that considers the theological significance and views of those outside the bounds of formal or official institutions.[25]

---

22. Muita, *Hewn from the Quarry*.
23. Muita, *Hewn from the Quarry*, 52.
24. Muita, *Hewn from the Quarry*, 81; Hastings, *History of African Christianity*, 238.
25. Ward, *Introducing Practical Theology*, 56.

It considers the everyday realities and stories of people as important sites of theological reflection.

Ward argues that "lived theology" is distinct from "lived religion," which has its roots in French sociology.[26] The distinction between the two is that religion usually mutes the theological ramifications of particular concepts or practices among communities by seeking to engage in a neutral gear.[27] Lived theology has emerged through the concepts of "ordinary theology" in the work of Astley and the movement of "the Four theological voices."[28] Its uniqueness is that it seeks to grapple with both the theological realities of Christian faith as well as the experiential aspects of Christian communities.[29] Additionally, Van den Toren explores the way in which lived theology sees Christian believers, in addition to academic texts, as important texts and "living documents" in themselves, particularly Western theological figures and texts, so as to expand theological reflection and its importance in the everyday life of ordinary Christian communities.[30] Thus, this chapter, following Ward's argument, unpacks lived theology as performative—that is to mean, how environmental theology, if there is such a concept among young people, is "enacted within everyday practices"[31] and whether or not there are conceptual or experiential aspects that guide or influence young people's faith. By mapping, this chapter will utilize a qualitative methodology to collect the insights from young Presbyterians and their engagement with the environment. This research seeks to unpack whether the church has played any role with raising the environmental awareness and action among young people, compared with the societal impetus when it comes to issues of environmental activism and advocacy, particularly within the framework of the African Union Agenda 2063.

Grounded in lived theology, this research focused on youth in the PCEA. The research used purposive sampling methods and used open-ended research interviews as the primary data collection method. I also engaged in informal interviews with key informants including a youth pastor who is a theological student researching ecological theology within the context of the PCEA. He mentioned a policy document from the PCEA

---

26. Ward, *Introducing Practical Theology*, 56.
27. Ward, *Introducing Practical Theology*, 63.
28. Ward, *Introducing Practical Theology*, 63.
29. Ward, *Introducing Practical Theology*, 63.
30. Van den Toren, "Researching African Lived Theology."
31. Ward, *Introducing Practical Theology*, 65.

that will be engaged in forthcoming sections as a secondary source of data. By and large, this study was qualitative and explorative in nature, and the following sections will use thematic coding to present the data emerging from the research correspondents. The qualitative approach is used as it seeks to listen attentively to young people in a "reflexive" way and to nurture Christian practices and virtues that lead to a full-orbed faith.[32] The assumption that guides this methodological approach is that, as Sensing says, "Human actions [and thoughts] are parts of God's economy."[33]

The research questionnaire was circulated among Presbyterian youth groups with responses received from February 9, 2023, to February 18, 2023. These groups included regional WhatsApp groups as well as the Presbyterian youth pastors WhatsApp group. After circulation, I analyzed the data and corrected for error. For instance, after receiving thirty total responses, I reduced them to twenty-seven because three of the responses were from those outside the youth bracket—two were forty years old and one was fifty-one years old. "Youth" in the PCEA is defined as those between the ages of thirteen and thirty-five years of age, which also fits in with the national definition in the key policy documents.[34]

Table 2 below presents a summary of the data emerging from the young people in the Presbyterian Church of East Africa.

Name (or initials)	Gender	Age	Parish name	Young people's role	Has Church helped?
JMO	Male	33	Eserian	EC	No
SRI	Male	32	Kiambu	EA - improvement	Neutral
CHC	Female	31	Banana Parish	EA - government engagement	Yes
JKR	Male	25	BANANA PARISH	EA - education	Yes
FDS	Female	24	Banana parish	EA - community awareness	Neutral
JNN	Male	30	Lari	EA - youth inclusion	No
SMW	Male	28	Banana	EA - improvement	Yes
SHN	Female	30	Banana	EA - improvement	Yes

32. Watkins, "Qualitative Research in Theology," 17.

33. Sensing, *Qualitative Research*, 12.

34. PCEA, *Practice and Procedure*; State Department for Youth, "Youth Development Policy."

Name (or initials)	Gender	Age	Parish name	Young people's role	Has Church helped?
JCB	Male	21	Ruiru	EA - youth inclusion	Yes
DRN	Male	26	Kaharati parish	EA - youth inclusion	Neutral
EWG	Female	22	Mbagathi Parish	EA - youth inclusion	Yes
WTH	Female	25	Lari	EA - mobilization	No
PN	Male	22	PCEA BANANA	EA - community awareness	Neutral
JSG	Male	23	JUJA		Yes
MNG	Male	28	Nanyuki	EA - youth inclusion	Neutral
KMW	Female	30	Githiga	EA - youth inclusion	Neutral
Mk	Male	25	Ebenezer	EA - community awareness	Yes
KGS	Male	25	Ngong parish	EA - advocacy	No
GWR	Female	30	Evergreen	EA - community awareness	No
NKW	Female	20	Bahati martyrs parish	EA - youth inclusion	Yes
MYT	Female	22	PCEA PANGANI	EA	Yes
SHK	Female	19	Kaharati/Kericho	EA - youth inclusion	No
SPN	Male	39	Ngecha	EA	Yes
JEL	Male	25	Ngecha	EA - advocacy	Yes
JC	Male	34	Ngecha Parish	EA - youth inclusion	Neutral
CRY	Female	20	Ngecha Parish	EA - community awareness	Yes
OMU	Male	20	Kamande parish		No

Table 2: Summary of Findings from Youth Survey on Ecotheology

EMERGING PRESBYTERIAN YOUTH VOICES ON ECOLOGICAL ISSUES

Youth Awareness of Ecological Issues

Although young people are usually construed as "leaders of tomorrow," the research revealed the knowledge resident among young people concerning environmental issues. Most of the respondents spoke about issues such as tree planting, afforestation, deforestation, poor farming methods, poor conservation methods, pollution, garbage disposal, climate change, greenhouse gas effects, among others. Some of the respondents revealed a sophisticated understanding of the global climate crisis, especially in its urgency, as well as the innovative approaches to solutions for environmental conservation and use. Some of the responses included the following:

> Adoption of green energy. With urbanization and congestion of population in the urban centres/growth of the population at large, land is diminishing and there is no large area to plant trees as it was a few years ago, therefore we need to be more innovative and think broadly on more ways other than tree planting. (KMW)

> Adoption of electric cars, which are more environmentally friendly and more conservative. (MK)

> The environmental issue I would consider as most important for our time is global warming. (MYT)

Beyond these thoughtful responses, Presbyterian youth also revealed an appreciation of the leadership and cultural factors that inhibit ecological responses in light of climate change crises. For instance, to the question, "What environmental issues or conversations would you consider as the most important for our time?" three different young people responded as follows:

> Technology
> Drug abuse/alcoholism
> Financial literacy
> Cultural beliefs
> Leadership and politics
> Marriage (JC)

> Educating members of church on issues like greenhouse effects; actually some don't believe in it. (CRY)

> Poor leadership (DRN)

The responses from young people support what has been discovered in the literature around the indirect factors that affect environmental change. The literature reveals that leadership styles, focus, and cultures have a direct correlation with responses to the ecological crises of our time, both in corporate organizations and communities in multireligious contexts.[35]

---

35. Torabi and Noori, "Religious Leaders," 351; Woo and Kang, "Environmental Issues," 16.

Youth Agency in Environmental Activism

The research revealed the important role that young people can play in leading ecological transformation and change. From the interviews, it was clear that young people consider the creative capacities and energies that they have in leading various engagements in light of the ecological crisis of our time. For example, some said,

> Educate the church on the importance of the environment exercise in environmental activities like tree planting, river cleaning, etc. Innovation; use latest technology to recycle waste products. (JKR)

> By having leadership positions in church; having open forums for the youths. (JC)

> The young people can help the church in environment issues by being key actors in the agenda of conserving the environment. This includes pitching and participating in environmental conservation campaigns and activities. (SHN)

Environmental knowledge and youth agency are undergirded by the fact that "environmental studies" is a compulsory subject in most undergraduate courses in Kenya's higher educational landscape. This follows The National Climate Change Act of 2016, which recommends the integration of climate change in university curricular as a strategy of climate change adaptation and mitigation.[36] While primary and secondary school teachers feel inadequate when it comes to climate change education, Ochieng' and Koske argue that if equipped, they can help learners move beyond passive engagement to action and policy change.[37]

The various ways in which young people consider their involvement when it comes to environmental action include:

- Advocacy
- Community awareness
- Education
- Government engagement
- Youth inclusion

---

36. Nyerere et al., "Kenya's Climate Change Policy," 9.
37. Ochieng and Koske, "Level of Climate Change."

Many respondents noted that young people should be included in their church's activities as well as in leadership. I have dealt elsewhere with the theme of "youth inclusion" within the context of the Presbyterian church, especially the mission context.[38] This research directly contributed to the thematic concern of youth agency when it comes to how young people in Africa function within the wider society. While the question was open-ended, some of the young people directly mentioned "leadership," thereby linking youth inclusion with environmental action by young people.

Employment Creation in the Environmental Sector

> By volunteering to support the community through tree planting, creating awareness on benefits of a healthy environment and holding campaigns to help the jobless youths realize their potential in job creation. All these activities will require funding from the church. (DRN)

> I personally have shaped the church fence as a contribution of my Christian worship. The youth usually rally behind leadership, but our contemporary churches hire workers to do all the work, thus denying youths an opportunity to engage in cleanup exercises or even compound beautification. Collaboration and a clear strategic plan with a benefit analysis needs to be worked on at congregational level to engage youths within their unique surroundings and urgent needs. (MK)

Emerging youth voices also reveal their perceived contribution to the high levels of youth unemployment. In Africa, one third of the 420 million young people are unemployed.[39] Muchira shows the opportunity that the cultural and creative industry (CCI) creates for absorbing the one million people entering Kenya's job market without any skills.[40] Given that churches are spaces that attract a number of young people, opportunities to use their creativity is a direct contribution to the youth unemployment dilemma. This research shows the resilience of young people in that, within the context of high unemployment, youth see themselves as "job creators," as DRN responded above. For MK, Christian life is not just a spiritual activity but directly correlates with their engagement in work: "I personally

---

38. Ndereba, "Let Them Come."
39. Muchira, "Digital Media," 168.
40. Muchira, "Digital Media," 169.

have shaped the church fence as a contribution of my Christian worship." Marginalization of young people is extracted from the response through their invisibility from the church's top leadership. Rather than utilizing their creativity, energy, and expertise, the church is accused of hiring external workers. Responding to ecological crises provides job opportunities for young people who are aware of the issues and have adequate capacities and tools to bring positive change to the community at large.

Young People Theologizing about the Environment

Only five Presbyterian youth said that they lack no biblical evidence for Christian engagement with the environment. Many of the respondents mentioned the creation narrative (Gen 1–2) as the central passage that supports environmental care. From this passage, respondents mentioned aspects such as,

- Creation care
- Dominion[41]
- Pollution
- Cleanliness

The majority of the respondents also revealed a decent and, in some cases, robust understanding of the biblical support for environmental stewardship.

> Yes, right from Gen 1 God created the world and saw that everything was good. This idea of God creating and making man a conserver is ideally the basis of every other idea in the Bible about environment. (JMO)
>
> Yes. Like dumping—it pollutes the air and dirties our compounds, especially in church; also the Bible tells us cleanliness is next to godliness. (CMC)
>
> Yes, the creation story depicts the human relationship with the environment. Man was given dominion over all the creation. Thus, if

---

41. There is a need to nuance the concept of "dominion" from what is popularly referred to as "dominion theology" within some neo-charismatic contexts that end up viewing the earth as something to be materially exhausted rather than as something that should be creatively explored. A fuller case is made in Ndereba, "Exploration of Pentecostal Theology."

> he has this dominion, then he ought to conserve the environment as a fulfillment of obeying God's commands. (EWG)

> We're called to take care of our environment and not to pollute it, just like our bodies. Deut 23:13-15; Jer 9:9-11; Hab 2:17; Lev 25:14; Gen 2:15; Gen 1:26-28; Num 35:33. (MWG)

Young people are familiar with their religious texts—not only the New Testament but also the Old Testament—as MWG shows us. Environmental conservation, according to GMC, is also a way of practicing Christian faith and "godliness." EWG eschews the dualistic interpretation of spirituality and materiality by situating human life within the context of a holistic worldview. According to this young person, ecological responses are an expression of one's relationship with God. From these few snapshots, we see young people as everyday theologians, everyday ecotheologians.

Resource Mobilization for Environmental Action

Young people are also cognizant of the fact that environmental action requires adequate resources to affect needed changes. One response, for example, noted the place of resource mobilization when it comes to responding to environmental concerns:

> Encourage the government to increase funding on the environmental sector. (CRY)

These ecological responses such as planting trees, utilizing green sources of energy, and changing farming practices require resources. Given the fact that young people, as earlier observed, lack employment opportunities and thus cannot access frequent funding, there is a need for both governmental organs and religious communities to support such "green initiatives" by young people. In this sense, environmental action is viewed not just an abstract utopia but as an enterprise that requires innovative solutions undergirded by resource mobilization.

THE CONTRIBUTION OF YOUTH LIVED ECOTHEOLOGY

The contribution of youth voices shows that ecotheology shapes our interaction with the environment. As much as we use our creative capacities to create new cultures, goods, and services, we must also "work it and keep [the land]."⁴² This eschews the excesses of a dominionistic approach to the environment by encouraging, for instance, good and equitable land use, taking care of our consumption and waste disposal, caring for our trees, and developing initiatives that lead to environmental sustainability. These activities open up spaces for employment creation, organizational advocacy, and business start-ups that have direct relevance for young people. For one, this ecosystem of environmental theology and praxis extends the space in which people practice faith. It embodies faith as an everyday concern that guides people on how to relate beyond self-centered pursuits and on engaging the people and environment around them—and also the generations and environments to come. Secondly, this ecosystem directly deals with the perversity of youth unemployment by harnessing the agency and fostering positive life outcomes for many young people who may not have access to work. Consequentially, as Cloete argues, this restores and sustains the dignity of young people in African and other contexts of the Global South.⁴³ Third, such an ecosystem emphasizes youth inclusion but also youth agency, thereby restoring the capacity for young people to develop and nurture their God-given skills, knowledge, and experience for the common good. This has direct bearing for young people to impact communities and societies for the welfare of nations.

RECOMMENDATIONS AND CONCLUSION

First, this chapter proposes that ecotheology be incorporated or integrated into theological curricula. It is understandable that pulpits lack an environmental concern, largely due to theological educational approaches that have been inherited and that continue on the lines of a sacred-secular divide that thrives on an enlightenment-oriented and individualistic ethos. This means that part of decolonizing theological education means addressing issues that affect us in our everyday realities. Given the inequalities surrounding the climate crisis, there is need to pay attention to how this affects the realities of Africans in various societies. Issues such as economic justice in the context of food insecurity must be engaged within theological education.

---

42. Other translations have a variation of the following words/phrases: "to tend and watch over it" (NLT); "to cultivate" (NASB), "to dress" (KJV), "to tend" (NKJV), "to watch over" (Holman), "to maintain" (NET); all capture various ecotheological nuances.

43. Cloete, "Youth Unemployment."

Second, there is need to translate ecotheology within communities of faith by incorporating the agency of young people. Young people already have the knowledge, skills, and ideas to respond to the contemporary global challenge of ecology. Churches can incorporate the leadership capacities of young people as teachers, preachers, content creators, and mobilizers for environmental causes. Ecotheology can be taught in a way that moves beyond planting of trees to capture how human greed correlates with environmental challenges and reflects negatively on our relationship with God, other people, and the world at large. Young people can direct efforts to translate the importance of the environment for the wider communities that they are a part of.

Third, this chapter proposes that ecotheological praxis is a vital way of restoring human dignity and fostering creative capacities of young people. The twenty-first century context means transformations across the workspace. In turn, environmental-oriented work across advocacy, education, community empowerment, government engagement, as well as conservation of biodiversity all provide tangible ways in which young people engage with the world and safeguard a habitable future.

This chapter reveals that theology must attend to the lived realities that face people. In our post-COVID context with significant concerns around climate change and food insecurity as a result of the economic situation, theology has something to contribute to the well-being of people. Also, this chapter reveals that young people have significant views around the environment, and while the church has helped them with interacting with their environment, there is much more that the church can do. Ecotheology or environmental theology remains critical as it is a tangible way we show our concern to what God has created—if we despise and destroy the created world, we are in essence despising and destroying the God who has created it. Additionally, environmental degradation is in essence our own degradation. Pushed to its limit, environmental degradation is an afront to and a denial of the future world and especially of the future generations coming after us. In the present, we are called to listen to youth voices who can help us lead the change.

10

Advocating for Youth and Economic Justice

THE COVID-19 PANDEMIC VALORIZES the marginality of young people from many fronts. Kenya is currently navigating adversity in climate change, especially through the drought present in many parts of the country. This drought further entrenches food insecurity and halts economic well-being and educational progress for young people. These factors create a dark present and future for Africa's youth. The Africa Union Agenda 2063 must seek economic well-being and empowerment for youth. What might theology have to say or contribute to the Africa that youth want? This chapter is grounded in practical theology and analyzes the Global Reformed Advocacy Platforms for Engagement (GRAPE) program, which is hosted by the World Communion of Reformed Churches (WCRC), in conjunction with the Economic Policy Research Institute (EPRI). This project was focused on economic justice within the Kenyan and South African context, and this research centers on youth voices, youth issues, and youth agency in the project. Additionally, this chapter engages biblical, ethical, and theological teaching on economic justice to further develop the normativity of economic justice. This chapter proposes that economic justice must be a category of youth ministry theory and praxis, especially for marginalized contexts that define much of the African continent, and will propose practical ways in which churches and Christian organizations can engage.

YOUTH AND THE TRIPLE PANDEMICS

Young people in African societies could be best described as sleeping giants. The "youth bulge" has generated significant interest in the past few decades. With the African population expected to triple by 2050, according to some estimates by the World Economic Forum (WEF),[1] the demographics as well as the contribution of young people is critical. However, while this creates potential promise quantitatively, the lived realities of young people create a qualitatively palpable hinderance. In Africa, most societies are embedded within a cultural hierarchy in which ancestors and the living dead are at the top of the sociocultural ladder, then elders in the society, the adult society, and finally children and young people. From such an understanding, young people are seen as the "leaders of tomorrow," whereby their sense of contribution and sense of agency is stifled, at best, and ignored, at worst. Additionally, the COVID-19 pandemic problematizes these marginalities, given the effect that the global pandemic has had on the economy and employment.

What this means is that while young people may have been adversely burdened in the various facets of their lived realities, the COVID-19 pandemic has increased the vulnerabilities of young people within various African contexts. The African Union Agenda 2063 rightly conceptualizes the problems but lacks a theological background that would safeguard a holistic approach to youth ministry, paying attention to concepts of economic greed, human dignity, and the promise of a future and hopeful world. What this calls for from ecclesial communities is a response that discerns this dire economic context and moves in practical action to offer a solution, what I term in this chapter "economic justice." Viewed this way, economic justice is seen as a viable youth ministry response given the triple pandemics—health, sociocultural, and political—facing young people today.

ECONOMIC JUSTICE THROUGH THE PRACTICAL THEOLOGICAL CYCLE

To address the viability of economic justice as a critical mode for youth ministry in our time, I utilize the practical theology cycle as an undergirding methodology. Figure 5 below represents the cycle as presented by Fuller Studios.[2]

1. World Economic Forum, "Africa," 9.
2. Fuller Studios, "Voices on Spiritual Formation."

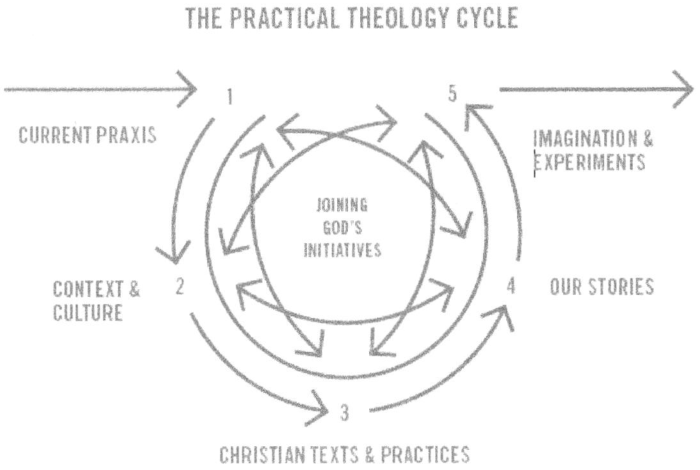

THE PRACTICAL THEOLOGY CYCLE

Figure 5: The Practical Theology Cycle

Practical theological methods move within various iterations that contemplate the interconnection of theory and praxis. The diagram above represents five key movements. Current praxis refers to our current mode of youth ministry—whereby much of our theologies, practices, and models of youth ministry are embedded within a dualistic separation of the spiritual and material.[3] Conceived this way, youth ministry is viewed as a practice of introducing people to Christ and growing them in maturity, without further engagement of their sociocultural and lived realities—factors that often impede this critical mission. Elsewhere, I have argued for more holistic forms of ministry.[4] This chapter focuses on economic justice as a specific model towards this holistic approach.

The second step in the practical theology cycle is to consider the context and culture embedded within our practices. From the foregoing presentation, this chapter has shown how young people today are affected by what is called the "triple pandemics." All through, this chapter notes the cultural context that young people within African contexts find themselves in and which merits theological reflection if youth ministry is to penetrate and transform the culture.

---

3. Aziz, "Public Practical Theology."
4. Ndereba, "Holistic Approach."

In the third step of the practical theology cycle, this chapter engages with a biblical and theological conceptualization of economic justice, as well as the practice of economic justice through the GRAPE program, which is hosted by the WCRC, in conjunction with the EPRI. This project was focused on economic justice within the Kenyan and South African context, and this chapter pays close attention to youth voices, youth issues, and youth agency in the project.

The fourth and fifth steps consider how the reflections from step one to three can be utilized to retell our stories of youth ministry as well as how they may innovate youth ministry practices in our continent. This validates practical theology as an interdisciplinary process of engagement between theory and praxis, which is central to the task of discerning our current realities in youth ministry reflection and practice. This chapter proposes that centering economic justice in our youth ministry practices will significantly enrich youth ministry in our societies as well as provide better models of practical theological reflection and research within the academy.

TOWARDS A BIBLICAL AND THEOLOGICAL PERSPECTIVE ON ECONOMIC JUSTICE

The role of socioeconomic transformation and development occupies the majority of reflection and work among scholars and practitioners in the academy and society. Economic justice is understood within the framework of development ethics that addresses the gaps raised in development theorizing and practice, both within the nationalistic bounds of societal and political factors but also within broader internationalizing contexts, including the frameworks and power dynamics of international organizations, business corporations, and states.[5] Economic justice is concerned with social issues, including inequality, fairness, equal opportunity, and upward mobility, among others.[6] Expanding this mode argues for a "global ethics" perspective whereby economic justice must be integrated with climate justice, environmental justice, and international justice, in addition to other justice frameworks.[7] This emphasis on integration is also proposed within the lens of Catholic Social Teaching (CST). CST emerges from the Roman Catholic tradition and reflection on how theology interfaces with social

---

5. Dower, "Global Ethics," 23–24.
6. Jimenez, *Social Policy*, 85.
7. Dower, "Global Ethics," 27.

theories and social institutions including church-state relations, the family, and the environment. One of the principles that CST teaches is the principle of subsidiarity whereby no institution is seen in isolation. Consequently, "speaking accurately about economic justice requires a precise understanding of institutions and their relationships to each other."[8] Thus, both developmental theory in specific developmental ethics as well as CST provide the conceptual foundation for thinking and practicing economic justice.

In the context of the GRAPE program, economic justice is interpreted as a theological issue. The theological underpinning of economic justice can be traced to the Accra Confession, which was a document resulting from consultations of the World Alliance of Reformed Churches (WARC) held at the twenty-fourth General Council in Accra, Ghana, in 2004. The conviction for the document arose from the fact that economic and environmental injustices required a response that was grounded in the gospel of Jesus Christ.[9] The wording around a "confession" follows the doctrine of confessions in the Reformed tradition, which have been premised on unity around matters of faith—and in this case, global justice issues such as the idols of mammon, consumerism, and authoritarian use of power that define contexts of suffering. Various biblical perspectives support this pursuit of issues of justice, including Old Testament texts (Gen 9:8–12; Ps 146:7–9; Isa 58:6; Mic 6:8; Amos 5:24) and New Testament texts (Matt 25:40; Luke 16:13; John 10:10; Rom 8:22). These passages explore the theological concepts of God covenanting with the whole of creation, the understanding of God as a God of justice, the calling of faith as expressed in acts of justice for the poor and oppressed, the expression of ministry as justice, mercy and care to all people, and God's vision for a whole and healed world. More specifically, the Pentateuch contains Scriptural injunctions to extend special care for the vulnerable through protecting resources for the poor from the rich (Deut 15:11; Lev 23:22; 25:25, 36–41). The rights of poor people are protected against unjust exploitation. Other New Testament passages expand this thinking for believers in the new covenant to express their love of God through love of neighbor, and especially in meeting the needs of those who are "weak" or poor (Mark 10:21; Acts 20:35; Gal 2:10; 1 Tim 6:18; Jas 2:5, 14–17). The Accra Confession interprets global realities of "oppression," "empire," "liberalization," and "neoliberal economics" as threats to

---

8. Heron and Ranganathan, "Catholic Social Teaching," 128.
9. World Alliance of Reformed Churches, "Accra Confession."

this ideal vision for all of creation.[10] Capturing the idea of economic justice, the Accra Confession posits in its nineteenth statement:

> Therefore, we reject the current world economic order imposed by global neoliberal capitalism and any other economic system, including absolute planned economies, which defy God's covenant by excluding the poor, the vulnerable, and the whole of creation from the fullness of life. We reject any claim of economic, political and military empire which subverts God's sovereignty over life and acts contrary to God's just rule.[11]

African theologians analyze this call for liberation and human dignity as part of the "prophetic discourse" of the church, which is central to the church's ministry in the context of neoliberal economic paradigms and can also be discerned in key theological documents such as the Kairos Document and the Oikos Journey.[12] In the South African context, the rise of black theology has been antecedent to these calls for more just socioeconomic and political systems.[13] Rathbone applies black theology in the reinterpretation or "reframing" of the Tower of Babel text, which was a primary text in the racial reading of the biblical narrative that supported apartheid in South Africa.[14] Koopman further explores the concept of justice as having both "sacrificial and forensic dimensions," which he interprets in light of the Belhar Confession: "People who are justified by the grace of God are participating in the quest of justice in the world."[15] This "compassionate justice" is directed towards others, and is seen practiced through sacrificing for others.[16] Such sacrificing will necessarily lead to the championing of human dignity, including socioeconomic rights in addition to the civil and political rights and developmental and environmental rights.[17] All these African theological models have been used to push for the well-being and dignity of all people, especially those who sit on the margins of society.

Given the "triple pandemics" affecting young people within the African context, economic justice must be an expression of Christian faith

---

10. World Alliance of Reformed Churches, "Accra Confession," 6.
11. World Alliance of Reformed Churches, "Accra Confession," 4.
12. Verhoef and Rathbone, "Economic Justice," 93.
13. Magezi and Tenai, "Black Theology," 61.
14. Rathbone, "Tower of Babel," 2.
15. Koopman, "On Violence," 163.
16. Koopman, "On Violence," 164.
17. Koopman, "On Violence," 166.

in search for dignifying the lives of our young covenant members.[18] To do this, these scholars argue, there is need to expand the understanding of the economy from just the material aspect to also include people, the environment, and their interactions. In the Kenyan context, this "prophetic discourse" has traversed the movements of inculturation, liberation, and reconstruction, and should now engage the economic arrangements of the Kenyan context. Following Moltmann, Tenai calls for the appropriation of public theology in addressing poverty: "Theology, in light of the hope in Christ, has to exhibit general concerns for the kingdom of God by being political in the name of the poor and marginalized."[19] Aziz uses the concept of public theology to expand the ministry of the church beyond an overly-spiritual and conversionist-only paradigm, to a paradigm that translates young people's lives and insights in the church's engagement.[20] Given the fact that many African societies, including the Kenyan context, are made up of young people without any social protection given the changing family landscape, economic justice as a mode of ministry by the community of faith is central—such family dynamics include fatherlessness, single-parent families, child-headed families, and blended families.[21] This chapter specifically focuses on economic justice as a way to do effective youth ministry in the context of the pandemic. The following section concludes the chapter with an analysis of how the GRAPE program has engaged in economic justice concerns.

ECONOMIC JUSTICE IN PRACTICE

The GRAPE program is a project hosted by the (WCRC), in conjunction with the EPRI.[22] This project invigorates the advocacy work of member churches in the communion, seeking solutions that connect global and local actors and responses. The work of GRAPE is inspired by the realization that churches have played a critical role in engaging with socioeconomic issues, and within the Global South, are respected by people in search of dignity. Thus, the role of churches is critical in extending an integral mission

---

18. Koopman and Smit, "Public Witness," 271; Verhoef and Rathbone, "Economic Justice," 94.
19. Tenai, "Enquiry on Poverty," 5.
20. Aziz, "Public Practical Theology," 6.
21. Ndereba, "Relevance of Covenant Theology," 86; Makiwane et al., "Children," 2.
22. World Communion of Reformed Churches, "Grape Pilot Project."

approach whereby mission is understood as a transformation of people's livelihoods in light of the gospel.

For the pilot project, there are two teams representing two countries—Kenya and South Africa. These two teams have been participating in both online and in-person trainings so as to design and develop advocacy campaigns working on specific social issues in the two countries. The South African team have designed a project on social protection through a government grant program and the Kenyan team have designed a project that will work on water scarcity through social policy. Both engagements are undergirded by theological convictions that seeks to address the inequality gaps in both countries by safeguarding the dignity of all people—especially those navigating poverty.

GRAPE seeks to build upon a project that was run by the WCRC in 2008–2009 called the Basic Income Grant (BIG), which was the first universal cash transfer project implemented globally. The BIG commenced in Otjivero, about one hundred kilometers east of Windhoek. All residents below the age of sixty years old received a BIG of N$100 per person per month, without any conditions attached.

In the context of the COVID-19 pandemic, there have been various governmental solutions to the dire circumstances affecting young people. For instance, one of the measures the previous Kenyan president Uhuru Kenyatta implemented to combat COVID-19 included a rollout of the National Hygiene Programme April 29, 2020. In a bid to deal with unemployment, this initiative was designed to employ 26,148 workers over thirty days and more than one hundred thousand youths progressively.[23]

Local churches and denominations also have a role to play. Youth and economic empowerment activities should be integrated in the youth ministry activities and programs so that young people in vulnerable contexts are equipped with skills and knowledge to respond to some of the challenges and opportunities around them. Dichotomizing youth ministry as a purely spiritual task is insufficient for working with young people on the underside of power and opportunities. Collaborations with professionals in congregations as well as partnerships with state actors and private companies can help to bridge the gap.

---

23. Gathogo, "COVID-19 Containment Measures," 130.

11

Peering into the Promising Future

THIS BOOK HAS MADE a simple argument. Faith formation activities with young people must move beyond the private sphere of faith to the public sphere of faith. Spiritual formational practices nurture a deep and long-lasting faith among young people. In the African context, these formational practices are grounded in the rich Christian tradition as well as the spiritual and cultural heritage that undergirds a variety of African contexts. However, a deep faith will also lead to a wider engagement with public life. What does this look like?

This book has made a further case for considering the Global South in our theological reflection. Moving beyond the thesis of Christianity moving to the Global South, this book shows how studying Christianity as conceptualized and practiced among young Africans is paramount to this task. However, contrasting with Western and other Global Northern contexts that are distinguished by generalized forms of individualism, young people in Africa still live within various communal contexts. While extended forms of family and kinship systems still define the contemporary realities of African youth, a new mode of virtual communalism exists within the digital contexts that shape much of African life today. Thus, conversations around discipleship, church, and mission must continue to grapple with the digital turn, which is especially pronounced in the post-COVID context. Thinking of church in both its nature and mission is critical for discerning contemporary forms of discipleship and missiology in a manner that creatively engages with the virtual reality so common in our life today.

Central to the task of youth ministry are the pastoral care tasks of sustaining, nurturing, and guiding. Pastoral care in the African context will continue to make use of the long tradition of *cura animarum*, i.e., care of souls, while navigating the new sociopolitical landscapes that define young people's lives, including and not limited to, sexual identification, youth unemployment, rising inequalities, and challenges on family systems. Despite the globalization changes affecting young people, pastoral care remains a critical ally in the forming tasks of Christian ministry, so central for continued public and prophetic engagement of and with young people.

Part of the public changes affecting contemporary life is the rise of conflicting narratives that pit faith and science as enemies. This book, anchored in a historical and social scientific analysis, has shown that this is a modern iteration of a much more nuanced discourse. Peering into the future, this book has shown that youth ministry will be called to a critical, constructive, and honest engagement between faith and science, right from the creation texts of the biblical narrative to the more practical concerns surrounding the questions of bioethics, in vitro fertilization, artificial intelligence, and biomedical engineering. This conversation will be critical in the Global South where science and development are entangled with a "strings attached" mentality of neo-colonial arrangements. This conversation is necessitated by African scientists who are at the cutting-edge of these developments as well as the growing demographic of young Africans taking science, technology, engineering, and mathematics (STEM) courses. These two important cohorts require a robust faith to engage and shape their scientific disciplines. The faith and science discourse will therefore not only safeguard the rigor of the Christian faith but also lead to more ethical, life-giving, and community-building scientific enterprises so critical for the Global South.

Climate change poses as one of these contemporary and global challenges. A central premise of the book has been to conceiving youth ministry from within a "global" context. This does not mean denigrating the place of local contexts shaping and informing global ideas and practices. Most of the chapters have grappled with these tensions of the local and global as a way of championing the idea of the "glocal." Climate change is one of the places where this is seen. A global reality, climate change does not only affect rural youth but also urban youth. Recent global reports on climate change disasters have focused on various regions of our globe and touched all the continents of our world. As such, while climate change adaptation and mitigation measures are championed, they will require a "glocal" approach. Such an approach rests on the solidarity of the global community working together to respond to the crisis, but also of specific and localized solutions needed for different climate change realities. This book has shown that young people are connecting their faith to these ecological concerns. A practical example of this is the Young Theologians Initiative for Climate Action (YTICA). Began as a youth-led group at the St. Paul's University School of Theology, the group has participated in the global ecumenical and secular discussions on climate change while designing practical responses for local public schools and faith communities in Kenya. This is an example of how, moving forward, faith must be connected with public realities such as climate change as a way of fully including the capacities, gifts, and energies of young people in communities of faith.

Finally, youth ministry must engage the economic realities that continue to hinder the development of young people in the Global South. Integral mission approaches that hold in good balance the spiritual and material realities, gospel proclamation, and gospel deeds will be needed in responding to the concerning inequalities that define many Global South societies.

This book has shown that the Christian heritage is both rich and diverse and is central in shaping the lives of young people who are a critical demographic in the world today. The demographic analyses available show that young people will continue to increase, proportional to wider society.[1] This will uniquely affect countries in the Global South, as the demographic changes within the Global North and West will not follow a steep trajectory of increase. What this means is that the present and future of the church is dependent on engagement with young people who require creative and long-term engagement from the rich resources of the Christian faith. While there are many concerns facing young people, this book argues that faith will remain a critical resource for the holistic well-being of young people in the present and future of our world today. While youth ministry approaches may require revitalization and rethinking, as this book has hopefully shown, youth ministry is here to stay.

---

1. Europe Commission, "Youth Bulges"; Ogunleye, "Leveraging Potentials."

Bibliography

Abbott, Dena M., and Debra Mollen. "Atheism as a Concealable Stigmatized Identity: Outness, Anticipated Stigma, and Well-Being." *The Counselling Psychologist* 46 (2018) 685–707.
Acolatse, Esther. *For Freedom or Bondage? A Critique of African Pastoral Practices.* Grand Rapids: Eerdmans, 2014.
Adedeji, Femi. "Christian Music in Contemporary Africa: A Re-Examination of Its Essentials." *Koers-Bulletin for Christian Scholarship* 72 (2007) 85–100.
AFIDEP. "Kenya Briefing Note: Regional Analysis of Youth Demographics." https://assets.publishing.service.gov.uk/media/5af9544740f0b622d7cc6e58/Kenya_briefing_note__Regional_Analysis_of_Youth_Demographics_.pdf.
African Union. "African Union Youth Charter." July 2, 2006. https://au.int/sites/default/files/treaties/7789-treaty-0033_-_african_youth_charter_e.pdf.
———. "Agenga 2063: the Africa We Want." https://au.int/en/agenda2063/overview.
Agang, Sunday Bobai, et al., eds. *African Public Theology.* Bukuru: Hippo, 2020.
Akpanessien, Anthony. "The Role of Pastoral Care and Guidance in the Spiritual Development of Postmodern Youth in Nigeria." PhD diss., University of Toronto, 2015.
Allen, Holly Catterton, and Christine Lawton. *Intergenerational Christian Formation: Bringing the Whole Church Together in Ministry, Community, and Worship.* Downers Grove, IL: InterVarsity, 2012.
Anderson, William H., ed. *Technology and Theology.* Wilmington, DE: Vernon, 2021.
Apollo, Abigael, and Marcellus Forh Mbah. "Challenges and Opportunities for Climate Change Education (CCE) in East Africa: A Critical Review." *Climate* 9 (2021) 1–16.
Arnett, Jeffrey Jensen. "Emerging Adulthood: What Is It, and What Is It Good For?" *Child Development Perspectives* 1 (2007) 68–73.
Arnett, Jeffrey Jensen, and Malcolm Hughes. *Adolescence and Emerging Adulthood.* Boston: Pearson, 2014.
Arweck, Elisabeth, and Heather Shipley, eds. *Young People and the Diversity of (Non) Religious Identities in International Perspective.* Berlin: Springer, 2019.
As, J. N. van. "Addressing the Phenomenon of Young South Africans Leaving the Church: A Practical Theological Investigation of the Role of Parents in Faith Formation." MA thesis, North-West University, 2021.

Bibliography

Asamoah-Gyadu, Kwabenah, et al. "The COVID-19 Pandemic and World Christianity." *Studies in World Christianity* 26 (2020) 213–18.

Ashamu, Christiana A. "Pastoral Care to Christian Youth in South Africa Who Experience Unwanted LGB Attraction." PhD diss., North-West University, 2020.

Augustine. *Confessions and Enchiridion*. Translated and edited by Albert C. Outler. Philadelphia: Westminster, 1955.

Avenant, Johan C., et al. "The Role of the Parental Home in the Intergenerational Faith Formation of the Youth for the Sake of an Integrated Youth Ministry." *Verbum et Ecclesia* 42 (2021) 1–11.

Awiti, Alex O., and Caleb Orwa. "Identity, Values and Norms of East Africa's Youth." *International Journal of Adolescence and Youth* 24 (2019) 421–37.

Aziz, Garth. "Environmental Justice as an Act of Love: A Reflection on the Agency of the Youth on the Cape Flats." *HTS Teologiese Studies/Theological Studies* 77 (2021) 1–6. https://doi.org/10.4102/hts.v77i2.6504.

———. "Youth Identity Discovery: A Theological Journey." *Pharos Journal of Theology* 100 (2019) 1–9.

———. "Youth Ministry as an Agency of Youth Development for the Vulnerable Youth of the Cape Flats." *Verbum et Ecclesia* 38 (2017) 1–6.

———. "Youth Ministry as a Public Practical Theology: A South African Evangelical Perspective." *HTS Teologiese Studies/Theological Studies* 78 (2022) 1–7.

Aziz, Garth, et al. "The Career Youth Pastor: A Contemporary Reflection." *HTS Teologiese Studies/Theological Studies* 73 (2017) 1–6. https://doi.org/10.4102/hts.v73i2.3856.

Baloyi, Magezi E. "Wife Beating Amongst Africans as a Challenge to Pastoral Care." *In die Skriflig* 47 (2013) 1–10.

Balswick, Jack O., et al. *The Reciprocating Self: Human Development in Theological Perspective*. Downers Grove, IL: InterVarsity, 2016.

Baron, Eugene. "Protecting Our Environment: The Need for South African Youth with a Mission and Black Consciousness." *HTS Teologiese Studies/Theological Studies* 77 (2021) 1–9. https://doi.org/10.4102/hts.v77i2.6740.

Barreto, Raimundo, and Fábio Py. "Ex- and Post-Evangelicalism: Recent Developments in Brazil's Changing Religious Landscape." *International Journal of Public Theology* 16 (2022) 197–222.

Bate, Stuart C. "Catholic Pastoral Care as a Response to the HIV/AIDS Pandemic in Southern Africa." *Journal of Pastoral Care & Counseling* 57 (2003) 197–209.

Bediako, Kwame. *Theology and Identity: The Impact of Culture upon Christian Thought in the Second Century and in Modern Africa*. Oxford: Regnum, 1999.

Berger, Peter L. *The Desecularization of the World: Resurgent Religion and World Politics*. Grand Rapids: Eerdmans, 1999.

Berkhof, Louis. *Systematic Theology*. Edinburgh: Banner of Truth Trust, 2012.

Best, R. E., et al. "Pastoral Care: Concept and Process." *British Journal of Educational Studies* 25 (1977) 124–35.

Bloesch, Donald G. *The Church: Sacraments, Worship, Ministry, Mission*. Downers Grove, IL: InterVarsity, 2002.

Bongmba, Elias. F., ed. *The Routledge Handbook of African Theology*. London: Routledge, 2020.

Bonhoeffer, Dieterich. *The Cost of Discipleship*. London: SCM, 1959.

———. *Discipleship*. Minneapolis: Fortress, 2003.

———. *Letters and Papers from Prison*. New York: Simon & Schuster, 1997.

Bibliography

Borgman, Dean. *Foundations for Youth Ministry: Theological Engagement with Teen Life and Culture.* Grand Rapids: Baker Academic, 2013.

Bosch, Tanja. "Twitter Activism and Youth in South Africa: The Case of #RhodesMustFall." *Information, Communication & Society* 20 (2016) 221–32. https://www.tandfonline.com/doi/full/10.1080/1369118X.2016.1162829.

———. "Twitter and Participatory Citizenship." In *Digital Activism in the Social Media Era: Critical Reflections on Emerging Trends in Sub-Saharan Africa*, edited by Bruce Mutsvairo, 159–73. Cham, Switzerland: 2016.

Bouwman, Kitty. "Spiritual Motherhood of Monica: Two Mothers in the Life of Saint Augustine." *Studies in Spirituality* 29 (2019) 49–69.

Boyo, Bernard. *The Church and Politics: A Theological Reflection.* Bukuru: Hippo, 2021.

Brake, Mike. *Comparative Youth Culture: The Sociology of Youth Cultures and Youth Subcultures in America, Britain, and Canada.* London: Routledge, 2013.

Branson, Mark Lau, and J. F. Martinez, eds. *Churches, Cultures, and Leadership: A Practical Theology of Congregations and Ethnicities.* Downers Grove, IL: InterVarsity, 2011.

———. "Practical Theology and Multicultural Initiatives." In *Churches, Cultures, and Leadership: A Practical Theology of Congregations and Ethnicities*, edited by Mark Lau Branson and J. F. Martinez, 33–58. Downers Grove, IL: InterVarsity, 2011.

Brink, Terry L. "Quantitative and/or Qualitative Methods in the Scientific Study of Religion." *Zygon: Journal of Religion and Science* 30 (1995) 461–75.

Bruin-Wassinkmaat, Anne-Marije de, et al. "Being Young and Strictly Religious: A Review of the Literature on the Religious Identity Development of Strictly Religious Adolescents." *Identity* 19 (2019) 62–79.

Brown, Don S. *A Fundamental Practical Theology: Descriptive and Strategic Proposals.* Minneapolis: Fortress, 1995.

Burbidge, Dominic. "'Can Someone Get Me Outta This Middle Class Zone?!' Pressures on Middle Class Kikuyu in Kenya's 2013 Election." *The Journal of Modern African Studies* 52 (2014) 205–25.

Calvin, John. *Institutes of the Christian Religion.* Edinburgh: Banner of Truth Trust, 2014.

Calvin Theological Seminary. "The Presidents of Calvin Theological Seminary." https://library.calvin.edu/hh/seminary-collection.

Campbell, Heidi A. *Digital Religion: Understanding Religious Practice in New Media Worlds.* London: Routledge, 2013.

———. "Introduction: Studying Digital Ecclesiology: How Churches Are Being Informed by Digital Media and Cultures." *Ecclesial Practices* 7 (2020) 1–10.

———, ed. *Digital Ecclesiology: A Global Conversation.* College Station, TX: Digital Religion. 2020. https://hdl.handle.net/1969.1/188698.

Campbell, Heidi A., and John Dyer, eds. *Ecclesiology for a Digital Church: Theological Reflections on a New Normal.* London: SCM, 2022.

Canales, Arthur D. "Ministry to Transgender Teenagers: Pursuing Awareness and Understanding About Trans Youth." *Journal of Pastoral Care & Counseling* 72 (2018) 195–201.

———. *Pastoral Care to and Ministry with LGBTQ Youth and Young Adults.* Eugene, OR: Wipf & Stock, 2022.

Carson, D. A. *Christ and Culture Revisited.* Grand Rapids: Eerdmans, 2012.

———. *Worship by the Book.* Grand Rapids: Zondervan, 2002.

Catto, Rebecca, and Janet Eccles. "(Dis)Believing and Belonging: Investigating the Narratives of Young British Atheists." *Temenos-Nordic Journal for Study of Religion* 49 (2013) 37–63.

Catto, Rebecca Alice, et al. "Diversification and Internationalization in the Sociological Study of Science and Religion." *Sociology Compass* 13 (2019) 1–13.

Chabata, Lovejoy. "Theological Education and Sustainable Development in Zimbabwe: Towards a Transformative Praxis in Doing Theology." In *A Critical Engagement with Theological Education in Africa: A South African Perspective*, edited by Johannes J. Knoetze and Alfred R. Brunsdon, 163–90. Cape Town: AOSIS, 2021.

Chan, Kwok-Bun, ed. *Hybrid Hong Kong*. London: Routledge, 2013.

Chancey, Dudley, and Ron Bruner. "A Reader's Guide to Intergenerational Ministry and Faith Formation." *Discernment: Theology and Practice of Ministry* 3 (2017) 59–78.

Chebukati, W. W. "Media Briefing." Independent Electoral and Boundaries Commission, June 20, 2022. https://www.iebc.or.ke/uploads/resources/JqmDO7vRLo.pdf.

Chiroma, Nathan. "Intergenerational Issues." In *African Public Theology*, edited by Sunday Agang et al., 353–64. Carlisle: Langham Publishing, 2020.

———. "The Role of Mentoring in Adolescents' Spiritual Formation." *Journal of Youth and Theology* 14 (2015) 72–90.

Chitando, Ezra. "Introduction: African Perspectives on Religion and Climate Change." In *African Perspectives on Religion and Climate Change*, edited by Ezra Chitando, et al., 1–21. London: Routledge, 2022.

Clark, Chap. *Hurt 2.0: Inside the World of Today's Teenagers*. Grand Rapids: Baker Academic, 2011.

Clark, Chap, ed. *Adoptive Youth Ministry (Youth, Family, and Culture): Integrating Emerging Generations into the Family of Faith*. Grand Rapids: Baker Academic, 2016.

Clarke, Peter, ed. *The Oxford Handbook of the Sociology of Religion*. Oxford: Oxford University Press, 2009.

Cloete, Anita. "The Church Is Moving On(line)." *Digital Ecclesiology: A Global Conversation* (2020) 27–31.

———. "Living in a Digital Culture: The Need for Theological Reflection." *HTS Teologiese Studies/Theological Studies* 71 (2015) 1–7. http://dx.doi.org/10.4102/hts.v71i2.2073.

———. "Revisiting a Family Approach in Youth Ministry." *In die Skriflig* 50 (2016) 1–6. https://dx.doi.org/10.4102/ids.v50i1.2078.

———. "Spiritual Formation as Focus of Youth Ministry." *NOMMERS* 3 and 4 (2012) 70–77.

———. "Youth Culture, Media and Sexuality: What Could Faith Communities Contribute?" *HTS Teologiese Studies/Theological Studies* 68 (2012) 1–6. http://dx.doi.org/10.4102/hts.v68i2.1118.

———. "Youth Unemployment in South Africa: A Theological Reflection Through the Lens of Human Dignity." *Missionalia: Southern African Journal of Mission Studies* 43 (2015) 513–25.

Cloete, Anita, ed. *Interdisciplinary Reflections on the Interplay Between Religion, Film, and Youth*. Stellenbosch: African Sun Media, 2019.

Collins, Úna M., and Jean McNiff, eds. *Rethinking Pastoral Care*. London: Routledge, 2012.

Comunello, Francesca, and Giuseppe Anzera. "Will the Revolution Be Tweeted? A Conceptual Framework for Understanding the Social Media and the Arab Spring." *Islam and Christian-Muslim Relations* 23 (2012) 453–70.

Bibliography

Conner, Benjamin T., and Rode Molla. "Youth Ministry Thought to an Ethiopian Context." *Journal of Youth Ministry* 16 (2018) 48–66.

Conradie, Ernst M. *Christianity and Ecological Theology: Resources for Further Research.* Stellenbosch: African Sun Media, 2006.

———. "The Four Tasks of Christian Ecotheology: Revisiting the Current Debate." *Scriptura: Journal for Biblical, Theological, and Contextual Hermeneutics* 119 (2020) 1–13.

Cotter, Christopher R. *The Critical Study of Non-Religion: Discourse, Identification, and Locality.* London: Bloomsbury, 2020.

Counted, Victor. "The Psychology of Youth Faith Formation: A Care-Giving Faith?" *Journal of Youth and Theology* 15 (2016) 146–72.

Cronshaw, D., et al. "Hemorrhaging Faith: An Australian Response in Exile." *Australian eJournal of Theology* 23 (2016) 14–31.

Cusic, Don, ed. *Encyclopedia of Contemporary Christian Music: Pop, Rock, and Worship.* London: ABC-CLIO, 2009.

Davies, Petronella J., and Yolanda Dreyer. "A Pastoral Psychological Approach to Domestic Violence in South Africa." *HTS: Theological Studies* 70 (2014) 1–8.

Dean, Kenda Creasy. *Almost Christian: What the Faith of Our Teenagers Is Telling the American Church.* Oxford: Oxford University Press, 2010.

———. *Practicing Passion: Youth and the Quest for a Passionate Church.* Grand Rapids: Eerdmans, 2004.

Deane-Drummond, Celia E. *A Primer in Ecotheology: Theology for a Fragile Earth.* Eugene, OR: Wipf & Stock, 2017.

Devellennes, Charles, and Paul Matthew Loveless. "The Tolerance of the Despised: Atheists, the Non-Religious, and the Value of Pluralism." *International Political Science Review* 43 (2022) 580–594.

DeYoung, Kevin, and Greg Gilbert. *What Is the Mission of the Church: Making Sense of Social Justice, Shalom, and the Great Commission.* Nairobi: Ekklesia Afrika, 2017.

Dixon, Thomas. *Science and Religion: A Very Short Introduction.* Oxford: Oxford University Press, 2008.

Dixon, Thomas, et al., eds. *Science and Religion: New Historical Perspectives.* Cambridge: Cambridge University Press, 2010.

Dower, Nigel. "Global Ethics." In *Routledge Handbook of Development Ethics*, edited by Jay Drydyk and Lori Keleher, 17–28. New York: Routledge, 2019.

Dreyer, Yolanda. "Reframing Youth: A Narrative and the Dream of a South African Idol." *Pastoral Psychology* 65 (2016) 643–55.

Ecklund, Elaine Howard, and David R. Johnson. *Varieties of Atheism in Science.* Oxford: Oxford University Press, 2021.

Elsdon-Baker, Fern. "Creating Hardline 'Secular' Evolutionists: The Influence of Question Design on Our Understanding of Public Perceptions of Clash Narratives." In *Identity in a Secular Age: Science, Religion, and Public Perceptions*, edited by Fern Elsdon-Baker and Bernard Lightman, 30–49. Pittsburgh: University of Pittsburgh Press, 2020.

Elsdon-Baker, Fern, and Will Mason-Wilkes. "The Sociological Study of Science and Religion in Context." In *Science, Belief, and Society: International Perspectives on Religion, Non-Religion, and the Public Understanding of Science*, edited by Stephen H. Jones et al., 3–24. Bristol: Bristol University Press, 2019.

Bibliography

Emery-Wright, Steven, and Ed Mackenzie. *Networks for Faith Formation: Relational Bonds and the Spiritual Growth of Youth*. Eugene, OR: Wipf & Stock.

Erikson, Erick Homburger. *Identity: Youth and Crisis*. New York: Norton, 1968.

Escobar, Samuel. *A Time for Mission: The Challenge for Global Christianity*. Carlisle: Langham, 2013.

Ess, Charles. "Digital Media Ethics." Oxford Research Encyclopedia of Communication, Sept. 26, 2017. https://oxfordre.com/communication/view/10.1093/acrefore/9780190228613.001.0001/acrefore-9780190228613-e-508.

Europe Commission. "Youth Bulges in Some Regions." Knowledge for Policy. Dec. 11, 2020. https://knowledge4policy.ec.europa.eu/foresight/topic/increasing-demographic-imbalances/youth_en.

Eze, Victor C., and Koblowe Obono. "The Influence of Internet Use on the Political Participation of Youth in Ikeja, Lagos." *Africology: The Journal of Pan African Studies* 11 (2018) 24–43.

Fazzino, L. L. "Leaving the Church Behind: Applying a Deconversion Perspective to Evangelical Exit Narratives." *Journal of Contemporary Religion* 29 (2014) 249–66. https://doi.org/10.1080/13537903.2014.903664.

Focer, Ada. "Frontier Internship in Mission: Researcher Statement by Ada Focer, PhD." Boston University School of Theology. https://www.bu.edu/sth/frontier-internship-in-mission-researcher-statement-by-ada-focer-phd/.

———. "The Frontier Interns Reenvisioned Missions for a Postcolonial Era." *The Christian Century*, Sept. 26, 2018. https://www.christiancentury.org/article/critical-essay/frontier-interns-reenvisioned-missions-postcolonial-era.

Focus Kenya. "49th FOCUS AGM, Annual Report." Apr. 8, 2022. https://www.focuskenya.org/wp-content/uploads/2022/04/FOCUS-AGM-Report-2022-Digital-Copy.pdf.

Foreign, Commonwealth, and Development Office. "Regional Analysis of Youth Demographics: A Briefing Report." May 11, 2018. https://www.gov.uk/research-for-development-outputs/regional-analysis-of-youth-demographics.

Forster, Dion A. "Reflecting on the Nature of Work in Contemporary South Africa: A Public Theological Engagement with Calling and Vocation." *HTS Theological Studies* 76 (2020) 1–10.

Fowler, James W. *Faith Development and Pastoral Care*. Minneapolis: Fortress, 2018.

———. *Stages of Faith: The Psychology of Human Development and the Quest for Meaning*. San Francisco: Harper & Row, 1981.

Frame, John. *Worship in Spirit and Truth*. Phillipsburg, NJ: P&R, 1996.

Freeks, Fazel. "Responding to the Challenge of Father Absence and Fatherlessness in the South African Context: A Case Study Involving Concerned Fathers from the North West Province." *Stellenbosch Theological Journal* 3 (2017) 89–113.

Fuller Studios. "Voices on Spiritual Formation." https://fullerstudio.fuller.edu/spiritual-formation/.

Gathogo, Julius. "COVID-19 Containment Measures and 'Prophecies' in Kenya." In *Religion and the COVID-19 Pandemic in Southern Africa*, edited by Fortune Sibanda et al., 126–41. New York: Routledge, 2022.

Gez, Yonatan N., et al. "African and Not Religious: The State of Research on Sub-Saharan Religious Nones and New Scholarly Horizons." *Africa Spectrum* 57 (2022) 50–71.

Gibson, Jonathan, and Mark Earngey. *Reformation Worship: Liturgies from the Past for the Present*. Greensboro, NC: New Growth, 2018.

Bibliography

Giroux, Henry A. *Youth in a Suspect Society: Democracy or Disposability?* New York: Palgrave Macmillan, 2009.

Glass, Jennifer L., et al. "Leaving the Faith: How Religious Switching Changes Pathways to Adulthood Among Conservative Protestant Youth." *Social Currents* 2 (2015) 126–43.

Gorski, Philip S., and Ateş Altınordu. "After Secularization?" *Annual Review of Sociology* 34 (2008) 55–85.

Government of Kenya. "Vision 2030 Development Strategy for Northern Kenya and Other Arid Lands." Food and Agriculture Organization of the United Nations, Mar. 2012. https://faolex.fao.org/docs/pdf/ken179242.pdf.

Graham, Elaine. "Is Practical Theology a Form of 'Action Research'?" *International Journal of Practical Theology* 17 (2013) 148–78.

Grobbelaar, Jan, and Gert Breed. *Welcoming Africa's Children: Theological and Ministry Perspectives.* Durbanville: AOSIS, 2016.

Haarmann, Claudia, and Dirk Haarmann. *Basic Income Grant: Otjivero, Namibia—10 Years Later.* Windhoek, Namibia: Economic and Social Justice Trust, 2019.

Hackett, Conrad, and Marcin Stonawski. "The Changing Global Religious Landscape." Pew Research Center, Apr. 5, 2017. https://www.pewforum.org/2017/04/05/the-changing-global-religious-landscape/.

Hall, G. Stanley. *Adolescence: Its Psychology and Its Relation to Physiology, Anthropology, Sociology, Crime, Sex, Religion, and Education.* New York: D. Appleton and Company, 1904.

Haste, Matthew. "So Many Voices: The Piety of Monica, Mother of Augustine." *The Journal of Discipleship and Family Ministry* 4 (2013) 6–10.

Hastings, Adrian. *A History of African Christianity 1950–1975.* Cambridge: Cambridge University Press, 1979.

Heitink, Gerben. *Practical Theology: History, Theory, Action Domains.* Grand Rapids: Eerdmans, 1999.

Heron, Jason A., and Bharat Ranganathan. "Catholic Social Teaching, Liberalism, and Economic Justice." *Journal of Moral Theology* 11 (2022) 126–46.

Hill, Jonathan P. *Emerging Adulthood and Faith.* Grand Rapids: Calvin College Press, 2015.

Hodkinson, Paul, and Wolfgang Deicke, eds. *Youth Cultures: Scenes, Subcultures, and Tribes.* New York: Routledge, 2007.

Howard, Jay R., and John M. Streck. *Apostles of Rock: The Splintered World of Contemporary Christian Music.* Lexington: University Press of Kentucky, 2014.

Innes, David C. *Christ and the Kingdoms of Men: Foundations of Political Life.* Phillipsburg, NJ: P&R, 2019.

Jacober, Amy E. *The Adolescent Journey: An Interdisciplinary Approach to Practical Youth Ministry.* Downers Grove, IL: InterVarsity, 2011.

Jenkins, Philip. *The Next Christendom: The Coming of Global Christianity.* Oxford: Oxford University Press, 2011.

Jimenez, Jillian. *Social Policy and Social Change: Toward the Creation of Social and Economic Justice.* Thousand Oaks, CA: Sage, 2010.

Jong, Jonathan. "On (Not) Defining (Non)Religion." *Science, Religion, and Culture* 2 (2015) 15–24.

Jun, Guichun. "Virtual Reality Church as a New Mission Frontier in the Metaverse: Exploring Theological Controversies and Missional Potential of Virtual Reality Church." *Transformation* 37 (2020) 297–305.

Bibliography

Kamau, Samuel C. "Democratic Engagement in the Digital Age: Youth, Social Media, and Participatory Politics in Kenya." *Communicatio* 43 (2017) 128–46. https://www.tandfonline.com/doi/abs/10.1080/02500167.2017.1327874.

———. "Engaged Online: Social Media and Youth Civic Engagement in Kenya." In *Digital Activism in the Social Media Era: Critical Reflections on Emerging Trends in Sub-Saharan Africa*, edited by Bruce Mutsvairo, 115–58. Cham, Switzerland: 2016.

Kapic, Kelly M. "Systematic Theology and Spiritual Formation: Encouraging Faithful Participation Among God's People." *Journal of Spiritual Formation and Soul Care* 7 (2014) 191–202.

Karanja, Lucy. "'Homeless' at Home: Linguistic, Cultural, and Identity Hybridity and Third Space Positioning of Kenyan Urban Youth." *Comparative and International Education* 39 (2010) 1–19.

Karp, Celia, et al. "Youth Relationships in the Era of COVID-19: A Mixed-Methods Study Among Adolescent Girls and Young Women in Kenya." *Journal of Adolescent Health* 69 (2021) 754–61.

Kaunda, Chammah J. "The Denial of African Agency: A Decolonial Theological Turn." *Black Theology* 13 (2015) 73–92.

Kenya National Bureau of Statistics. "2019 Kenya Population and Housing Census, Vol 4: Distribution of Population by Socio-Economic Characteristics." Dec. 2019. https://www.knbs.or.ke/wp-content/uploads/2023/09/2019-Kenya-population-and-Housing-Census-Volume-4-Distribution-of-Population-by-Socio-Economic-Characteristics.pdf.

———. "Kenya Demographic and Health Survey 2014." Dec. 2015. https://dhsprogram.com/pubs/pdf/fr308/fr308.pdf.

Khalema, Nene Ernest, et al., eds. *Children in South African Families: Lives and Times*. Cambridge: Cambridge Scholars, 2016.

Kimari, W., et al. "Youth, the Kenyan State, and a Politics of Contestation." *Journal of Eastern African Studies* 14 (2020) 690–706.

Kinnaman, David, and Aly Hawkins. *You Lost Me: Why Young Christians are Leaving Church . . . and Rethinking Faith*. Grand Rapids: Baker, 2011.

Kinnaman, David, and Gabe Lyons. *UnChristian: What a New Generation Really Thinks About Christianity . . . and Why It Matters*. Grand Rapids: Baker, 2007.

Kirk TV Kenya. "The 23rd General Assembly of the Presbyterian Church of East Africa." PCEA, Apr. 6 2021. https://www.facebook.com/watch/live/?v=1153413335119208&ref=search.

Kirkpatrick, David C. "C. René Padilla and the Origins of Integral Mission in Post-War Latin America." *The Journal of Ecclesiastical History* 67 (2016) 351–71.

———. *A Gospel for the Poor: Global Social Christianity and the Latin American Evangelical Left*. Philadelphia: University of Pennsylvania Press, 2019.

Klaasen, John S. "Practical Theology: A Critically Engaged Practical Reason Approach of Practice, Theory, Practice, and Theory." *HTS Teologiese Studies/Theological Studies* 70 (2014) 1–6. http://dx.doi.org/10.4102/hts.v70i2.1950.

Knoetze, Johannes J. "Marginalized Millennials: Conversation or Conversion Towards a Christian Lifestyle in South Africa?" *HTS Teologiese Studies/Theological Studies* 74 (2018) 1–7. https://doi.org/10.4102/hts.v74i3.4999.

Koopman, Nico. "On Violence, the Belhar Confession, and Human Dignity." *Nederduitse Gereformeerde teologiese Tydskrif/Dutch Reformed Theological Journal* 49 (2008) 159–66.

Bibliography

Koopman, Nico, and Dirkie Smit. "Public Witness in the Economic Sphere? On Human Dignity as a Theological Perspective." In *Christian in Public. Aims, Methodologies, and Issues in Public Theology*, edited by Len Hansen, 269–80. Stellenbosch: Sun Media, 2007.

Köstenberger, Andreas J., and David W. Jones. *God, Marriage, and Family: Rebuilding the Biblical Foundation*. 2nd ed. Wheaton, IL: Crossway, 2010.

Kraft, Charles H. *Issues in Contextualization*. Pasadena, CA: William Carey Library, 2016.

Kritzinger, Johannes. "Church and Development." *Scriptura: Journal for Biblical, Theological, and Contextual Hermeneutics* 39 (1991) 15–24.

Larsen, Timothy, and Daniel J. Treier, eds. *The Cambridge Companion to Evangelical Theology*. Cambridge: Cambridge University Press, 2007.

Lartey, Emmanuel Y. *In Living Color: An Intercultural Approach to Pastoral Care and Counselling*. Philadelphia: Jessica Kingsley, 2003.

Lee, Lois. "Ambivalent Atheist Identities: Power and Non-Religious Culture in Contemporary Britain." *Social Analysis* 59 (2015) 20–39.

———. *Recognizing the Non-Religious: Reimagining the Secular*. Oxford: Oxford University Press, 2015.

Leicht, Carola, et al. "Content Matters: Perceptions of the Science-Religion Relationship." *The International Journal for the Psychology of Religion* 32 (2021) 232–55.

Lindhardt, Martin. "'We, the Youth, Need to be Effusive': Pentecostal Youth Culture in Contemporary Chile." *Bulletin of Latin American Research* 31 (2012) 485–98.

Liu, Yen-Chin, et al. "COVID-19: The First Documented Coronavirus Pandemic in History." *Biomedical Journal* 43 (2020) 328–33.

Longman, Timothy. *Christianity and Genocide in Rwanda*. Cambridge: Cambridge University Press, 2010.

Lukalo, Fibian Kavulani. *Extended Handshake or Wrestling Match? Youth and Urban Culture Celebrating Politics in Kenya*. Uppsala: Nordiska Afrikainstitutet, 2006.

Maddix, Mark A., et al. *Understanding Faith Formation: Theological, Congregational, and Global Dimensions*. Grand Rapids: Baker Academic, 2020.

Madge, Nicola, et al. *Youth on Religion: The Development, Negotiation, and Impact of Faith and Non-Faith Identity*. London: Routledge, 2014.

Magesa, Laurenti. *African Religion: The Moral Traditions of Abundant Life*. Maryknoll, NY: Pauline, 1997.

Magezi, Vhumani. "Practical Theology in Africa: Situation, Approaches, Framework and Agenda Proposition." *International Journal of Practical Theology* 23 (2019) 115–35. https://www.degruyterbrill.com/document/doi/10.1515/ijpt-2018-0061/html.

———. "Public Pastoral Care as Nexus and Opportunity for a Transformed Practical Theology Within Decolonization Discourse in South African Higher Education." *In die Skriflig* 52 (2018) 1–10.

———. "Reflection on Pastoral Care in Africa: Towards Discerning Emerging Pragmatic Pastoral Ministerial Responses." *In die Skriflig* 50 (2016) 1–7.

Magezi, Vhumani, and Noah K. Tenai. "Black Theology and Its Response to Poverty in the Public Sphere—A Case for the Africa Inland Church in Kenya." *Black Theology* 15 (2017) 60–78.

Maina, Charles M. "Challenges of Ministering to the Youth: A Case Study of Presbyterian Church of East Africa Langata Parish, Nairobi County." MA thesis, University of Nairobi, 2015.

Bibliography

Mamati, King'asia, and Loreen Maseno. "Environmental Consciousness Amongst Indigenous Youth in Kenya: The Role of the Sengwer Religious Tradition." *HTS Teologiese Studies/Theological Studies* 77 (2021) 1–10.

Marti, Gerardo, and Gladys Ganiel. *The Deconstructed Church: Understanding Emerging Christianity*. Oxford: Oxford University Press, 2014.

Marvasti, Amir. *Qualitative Research in Sociology*. London: Sage, 2004.

Masango, Maake J. S. "African Spirituality that Shapes the Concept of Ubuntu." *Verbum et Ecclesia* 27 (2006) 930–43.

Mason-Wilkes, Will. "Divine DNA? 'Secular' and 'Religious' Representations of Science in Nonfiction Science Television Programs." *Zygon: Journal of Religion and Science* 55 (2020) 6–26.

Maseno, Loreen, and King'asia Mamati. "An Appraisal of the Pentecostal Eco-Theology and Environmental Consciousness Among Youths in Parklands Baptist Church, Kenya." *HTS Teologiese Studies/Theological Studies* 77 (2021) 1–7.

Mbiti, John. *African Religions and Philosophy*. Nairobi: Heinemann, 1990.

———. *Concepts of God in Africa*. London: SPCK, 1970.

McNamara, Barry, et al. "Religiosity and Spirituality During the Transition to Adulthood." *International Journal of Behavioral Development* 34 (2010) 311–24.

Merriam, Sharan B., and Elizabeth J. Tisdell. *Qualitative Research: A Guide to Design and Implementation*. San Francisco: Jossey-Bass, 2016.

Metaxas, Eric. *Bonhoeffer: Pastor, Martyr, Prophet, Spy*. Nashville: Thomas Nelson, 2010.

Miano, Rebecca. "Press Statement on Drought Situation in the Country." Ministry of East African Community, the ASALs, and Regional Development, Jan. 11, 2023. https://ndma.go.ke/download/press-release-drought-update-january-2023/.

Milemba, Elina K. "The Influence of Prosperity Gospel on the Well-Being of Youth: A Contemporary Study of Christian Churches." MA thesis, University of Nairobi, 2015.

Mohamed, Miraji Hassan. "Dangerous or Political? Kenyan Youth Negotiating Political Agency in the Age of 'New Terrorism.'" *Media, War, and Conflict* 14 (2021) 303–21.

Molteni, Francesco. *A Need for Religion: Insecurity and Religiosity in the Contemporary World*. Leiden: Brill, 2020.

Mucherera, Tapiwa N. *Counseling and Pastoral Care in African and Other Cross-Cultural Contexts*. Eugene, OR: Wipf & Stock, 2017.

Mucherera, Tapiwa N., and Emmanuel Lartey, eds. *Pastoral Care, Health, Healing, and Wholeness in African Contexts: Methodology, Context, and Issues*. Eugene, OR: Wipf & Stock, 2017.

Muchira, John Munyui. "Digital Media and Creative Economy Potential on Youth Employment in Kenya: A Grounded Theory Perspective." *Information and Learning Sciences* 124 (2023) 168–93.

Mudge, Melanie. "What Is Faith Deconstruction?" The Sophia Society, Mar. 7, 2021. https://www.sophiasociety.org/blog/what-is-faith-deconstruction.

Mueller, Walt. *Engaging the Soul of Youth Culture: Bridging Teen Worldviews and Christian Truth*. Downers Grove, IL: InterVarsity, 2006.

Mugambi, J. N. K., and Laurenti Magesa, eds. *The Church in African Christianity*. Nairobi: Initiatives, 1990.

Muggleton, David, and Rupert Weinzierl, eds. *The Post-Subcultures Reader*. Oxford: BERG, 2003.

Muita, Isaiah Wahome. *Hewn from the Quarry: The Presbyterian Church of East Africa 100 Years and Beyond*. Nairobi: PCEA Jitegemea, 2003.

Bibliography

Mukhongo, Lynete Lusike. "Participatory Media Cultures: Virality, Humour, and Online Political Contestations in Kenya." *Africa Spectrum* 55 (2020) 148–69.

Mulholland, M. Robert. *Invitation to a Journey: A Road Map for Spiritual Formation.* Downers Grove, IL: InterVarsity, 2016.

Müller, Julian. "Postfoundational Practical Theology for a Time of Transition." *HTS Teologiese Studies/Theological Studies* 67 (2011) 1–5. https://hts.org.za/index.php/hts/article/view/837.

———. "Practical Theology as Part of the Landscape of Social Sciences and Humanities: A Transversal Perspective." *HTS Teologiese Studies/Theological Studies* 69 (2013) 1–5. http://dx.doi.org/10.4102/hts.v69i2.1299.

Munyao, Martin, ed. *The African Church and COVID-19: Human Security, the Church, and Society in Kenya.* Lanham, MD: Lexington, 2022.

Mutsvairo, Bruce, ed. *Digital Activism in the Social Media Era: Critical Reflections on Emerging Trends in Sub-Saharan Africa.* Cham, Switzerland: Palgrave Macmillan, 2016.

Mwambazambi, Kalemba. "A Missiological Reflection on African Ecclesiology." *Verbum et Ecclesia* 32 (2011) 1–8.

Mwabe, Julie, et al. "Promises to Keep: Impact of COVID-19 on Adolescents in Kenya." Presidential Policy and Strategy Unit, June 24, 2021. https://knowledgecommons.popcouncil.org/cgi/viewcontent.cgi?article=2378&context=departments_sbsr-pgy.

Mwangi, Charles M. "Challenges of Ministering to the Youth: A Case Study of Presbyterian Church of East Africa Langata Parish, Nairobi County." MA thesis, University of Nairobi, 2015.

Naidoo, Marilyn. "Overcoming Alienation in Africanising Theological Education." *HTS Theological Studies* 72 (2016) 1–8.

Ndereba, Kevin Muriithi. "Emerging Themes in Apologetics for Contemporary African Youth Ministry." *Stellenbosch Theological Journal* 8 (2022) 1–18.

———. "Environmental Justice and Ecumenism: The Lacuna in African Christianity." *The Ecumenical Review* 73 (2021) 524–34.

———. "An Exploration of Pentecostal Theology and Praxis of Salvation in Kenya." In *Salvation in African Christianity*, edited by Rodney Reed and David Ngaruiya, 381–400. Carlisle: Langham, 2023.

———. "Faith, Science, and Nonreligious Identify Formation Among Male Kenyan Youth." *Zygon* 58 (2023) 45–63.

———. "A Holistic Approach to Youth Ministry Models in Africa: A Practical Theology for Faith Formation." *Journal of Youth and Theology* 22 (2023) 66–77.

———. "Let Them Come to Me: A Youth Inclusive and Missional Perspective in Presbyterian Context." *Journal of Youth and Theology* 21 (2021) 45–57.

———. "The Relevance of Covenant Theology to Fatherlessness in Kenya: A Youth and Family Ministry Perspective." *Acta Theologica* 42 (2022) 84–97. http://dx.doi.org/10.18820/23099089/actat.v42i1.6.

———. "The Role of Youth Culture in Holistic Faith Formation of Youth in Nairobi: A Practical Theological Approach." PhD diss., University of South Africa, 2021.

———. "Toward a Theology of Creation: An African Approach to the Environment. In *God and Creation*, edited by David Ngaruiya and Rodney Reed, 83–96. Bukuru: Langham, 2019.

———. "Towards a Kenyan Political Theology: The Importance of Church History for Contemporary Public Life." *African Journal of History and Culture* 13 (2021) 102–9.

———. "Ubuntu Apologetics in Faith Formation: An Ethnography of Youth Ministry in Nairobi." *Journal of Youth and Theology* 1 (2021) 1–16.

———. "Youth Transitions During the Pandemic: An Empirical Approach." In *The Palgrave Handbook of Global Social Change*, edited by Rajendra Baikady et al., 1–13. London: Palgrave Macmillan, 2024. https://link.springer.com/rwe/10.1007/978-3-030-87624-1_251-1.

———. "Youth Worldviews Among the De-Churched in Nairobi and Implications for Ministry." MA thesis, International Leadership University, 2015.

Nel, Malan. "Imagine-Making Disciples in Youth Ministry . . . That Will Make Disciples." *HTS Teologiese Studies/Theological Studies* 71 (2015) 1–11. http://dx.doi.org/10.4102/hts.v71i3.2940.

———. *Youth Ministry: An Inclusive Missional Approach*. Cape Town: AOSIS, 2018.

———. "Youth Ministry as a Practical Theology: Making a Case for Youth Ministry as an Academic Discipline." *Journal of Youth and Theology* 2 (2003) 68–83.

Nel, Reggie W. "Social Media and the New Struggles of Young People Against Marginalization: A Challenge to Missional Ecclesiology in Southern Africa." *Stellenbosch Theological Journal* 1 (2015) 511–30. http://dx.doi.org/10.17570/stj.2015.v1n2.a24.

Nichols, James H. *Corporate Worship in the Reformed Tradition*. Eugene, OR: Wipf & Stock, 2014.

Niebuhr, H. Richard. *Christ and Culture*. New York: Harper & Row, 1951.

Niemelä, K. "'No Longer Believing in Belonging': A Longitudinal Study of Finnish Generation Y from Confirmation Experience to Church-Leaving." *Social Compass* 62 (2015) 172–86.

Njoya, Timothy. *We the People: Thinking Heavenly, Acting Kenyanly*. Nairobi: WordAlive, 2017.

Ntarangwi, Mwenda. *East African Hip Hop: Youth Culture and Globalization*. Chicago: University of Illinois Press, 2009.

———. *The Street Is My Pulpit: Hip Hop and Christianity in Kenya*. Chicago: University of Illinois Press, 2016.

Nyakwara, Peter A., et al. "The State of Kenya Population." National Council for Population and Development, June 2020. https://kenya.unfpa.org/sites/default/files/pub-pdf/state_of_kenya_population_report_2020.pdf.

Nyamiti, Charles. "The Church as Christ's Ancestral Mediation: An Essay on African Ecclesiology." In *The Church in African Christianity: Innovative Essays in Ecclesiology*, edited by J. N. K. Mugambi and Laurenti Magesa, 129–77. Nairobi: Initiatives, 1990.

Nyerere, Jackline, et al. *Kenya's Climate Change Policy Actions and the Response of Higher Education*. Transforming Universities for a Changing Climate, Working Paper Series 4. London: University College of London, 2021.

Ochieng, Millicent A., and James Koske. "The Level of Climate Change Awareness and Perception Among Primary School Teachers in Kisumu Municipality, Kenya." *International Journal of Humanities and Social Science* 3 (2013) 174–79.

O'Connor, Paul. "Everyday Hybridity and Hong Kong's Muslim Youth." In *Hybrid Hong Kong*, edited by Kwok-Bun Chan, 250–72. London: Routledge, 2012.

Ogden, Greg. "The Discipleship Deficit: Where Have All the Disciples Gone?" *Knowing and Doing* 2 (2011) 1–5.

Ogola, George. "#Whatwouldmagufulido? Kenya's Digital 'Practices' and 'Individuation' as a (Non) Political Act." *Journal of Eastern African Studies* 13 (2019) 124–39.

Bibliography

Ogunleye, Eric K. "Leveraging Potentials of the Youth for Inclusive, Green, and Sustainable Development in Africa." https://www.afdb.org/sites/default/files/2023/08/11/setting_the_scene_presentation_for_g-cop_on_youth_s_.pdf.

Okoth, Grace Brenda W. "How Kenyans on Twitter Use Visuals as a Form of Political Protest." *Journal Kommunikation Medien* 12 (2020) 1–27.

Okwuosa, Lawrence N., et al. "Double Denominational Belonging Among Youths in Nigeria: Implications on Christianity." *Journal of Youth and Theology* 19 (2020) 95–114.

Olagunju, A., et al. "Beyond #FeesMustFall: Understanding the Inclusion Role of Social Media During Students' Protests in South Africa." *Cogent Education* 9 (2022) 1–12.

Old, Hughes O. *Worship: Reformed According to Scripture*. Louisville: Westminster John Knox, 2002.

Orevillo-Montenegro, M. "Eco-Feminism and Eco-Feminist Theology." In Louk Andrianos et al., eds. *Reclaiming Earth-Based Spirituality. Kairos for Creation: Confessing Hope for the Earth: The "Wuppertal Call"—Contributions and Recommendations from an International Conference on Eco-Theology and Ethics of Sustainability*, 235–42. Solingen: WCC, 2019.

Orobator, Agbonkhianmeghe E. "Perspectives and Trends in Contemporary African Ecclesiology." *Studia Missionalia* 45 (1996) 267–81.

———. *Religion and Faith in Africa: Confessions of an Animist*. Maryknoll, NY: Orbis, 2021.

Osmer, Richard R. *Practical Theology: An Introduction*. Grand Rapids: Eerdmans, 2008.

Osmer, Richard R., and Katherine M. Douglass. *Cultivating Teen Faith: Insights from the Confirmation Project*. Grand Rapids: Eerdmans, 2018.

Palfrey, John, and Urs Gasser. *Born Digital: How Children Grow Up in a Digital Age*. New York: Basic, 2016.

Parliament of Kenya. "Kenya Constitution, 2010." https://kenyalaw.org/kl/fileadmin/pdfdownloads/TheConstitutionOfKenya.pdf.

Parrett, Gary A., and S. Steve Kang. *Teaching the Faith, Forming the Faithful: A Biblical Vision for Education in the Church*. Downers Grove, IL: InterVarsity, 2009.

Patton, John. *Pastoral Care in Context: An Introduction to Pastoral Care*. Louisville: Westminster John Knox, 2005.

PCEA. "The Report of the Central Youth Committee (CYC) to the 22nd General Assembly." Nairobi, PCEA: 2018.

———. *Practice and Procedure*. Nairobi: Jitegemea, 1998.

Pike, Isabel, et al. "Making Sense of Marriage: Gender and the Transition to Adulthood in Nairobi, Kenya." *Journal of Marriage and Family* 80 (2018) 1298–313.

Population Council. "Promises to Keep: Impact of COVID-19 on Adolescents in Kenya." June 24, 2021. https://knowledgecommons.popcouncil.org/cgi/viewcontent.cgi?article=2378&context=departments_sbsr-pgy

Purves, Andrew. *Pastoral Theology in the Classical Tradition*. Louisville: Westminster John Knox, 2001.

Ramsay, Nancy J., ed. *Pastoral Theology and Care: Critical Trajectories in Theory and Practice*. New York: Wiley & Sons, 2018.

Rathbone, Mark. "Reframing the Tower of Babel Narrative for Economic Justice Within the South African Context." *HTS: Theological Studies* 72 (2016) 1–9.

Bibliography

Resnick, Danielle, and Daniela Casale. "The Political Participation of Africa's Youth: Turnout, Partisanship, and Protest." World Institute for Development Economics Research, Sept. 2011. https://www.econstor.eu/handle/10419/54172.

Roberts, Robert C. *Spirituality and Human Emotion*. Grand Rapids: Eerdmans, 1982.

Root, Andrew. *Faith Formation in a Secular Age: Responding to the Church's Obsession with Youthfulness*. Grand Rapids: Baker Academic, 2017.

———. *Revisiting Relational Youth Ministry: From a Strategy of Influence to a Theology of Incarnation*. Downers Grove, IL: InterVarsity, 2007.

Root, Andrew, and Kenda Creasy Dean. *The Theological Turn in Youth Ministry*. Downers Grove, IL: InterVarsity, 2011.

Ruso, Domenic. "Reflections of a Church Planter: Digital Natives and the Shaping of a Church to Come." *Post-Christendom Studies* 3 (2019) 111–27.

Sabar, Galia. *Church, State, and Society in Kenya: From Mediation to Opposition, 1963–1993*. London: Frank Cass, 2002.

Sakupapa, Teddy Chalwe. "The Decolonising Content of African Theology and the Decolonisation of African Theology: Reflections on a Decolonial Future for African Theology." *Missionalia: Southern African Journal of Mission Studies* 46 (2018) 406–24.

Sanneh, Lamin. *Translating the Message: The Missionary Impact on Culture*. Maryknoll, NY: Orbis, 2015.

Sauti Sol and Aaron Rimbui. "Kuliko Jana." *Live and Die in Afrika*. Track 11. 2015.

Sauti Sol and Nyashinkski. "Short N Sweet." *Afrikan Sauce*. Track 5. 2019.

Selvam, S. G. *Empirical Research*. Nairobi: Pauline, 2017.

Sensing, Tim. *Qualitative Research: A Multi-Methods Approach to Projects for Doctor of Ministry Dissertations*. Eugene, OR: Wipf & Stock, 2022.

Senter, Mark. *Four Views of Youth Ministry and the Church: Inclusive Congregational, Preparatory, Missional, Strategic*. Grand Rapids: Zondervan, 2001.

———. *When God Shows Up: A History of Protestant Youth Ministry in America*. Grand Rapids: Baker Academic, 2010.

Setran, David P., and Chris A. Kiesling. *Spiritual Formation in Emerging Adulthood: A Practical Theology for College and Young Adult Ministry*. Grand Rapids: Baker Academic, 2013.

ShahidiHub Africa. "Shahidihub Research Poll Release on 'The State of the Church in Kenya After Phased Reopening.'" Mar. 27, 2021. https://shahidihub.wordpress.com/2021/03/27/a-poll-release-on-the-state-of-the-church-in-kenya-after-phased-reopening-of-churches/.

———. "Shahidihub Research Poll Release: The State of the Church in Kenya During the Covid-19 Pandemic." June 26, 2020. https://shahidihub.wordpress.com/2020/06/26/poll-release-the-state-of-the-church-in-kenya-during-the-covid-19-pandemic-download/.

Singleton, Andrew, et al. "Spirituality in Adolescence and Young Adulthood: A Method for a Qualitative Study." *International Journal of Children's Spirituality* 9 (2004) 247–62.

Smit, Dirk J. "On the Reception of Bonhoeffer: A Case Study of South-South Dialogue." *Stellenbosch Theological Journal* 2 (2016) 89–107. http://dx.doi.org/10.17570/stj.2016.v2n1.a05.

Smith, Christian, and Melina Lundquist Denton. *Soul Searching: The Religious and Spiritual Lives of American Teenagers*. Oxford: Oxford University Press, 2009.

Smith, James K. A. *Desiring the Kingdom: Worship, Worldview, and Cultural Formation*. Grand Rapids: Baker Academic, 2009.

Bibliography

Smith, Kay Higuera, et al., eds. *Evangelical Postcolonial Conversations: Global Awakenings in Theology and Praxis*. Downers Grove, IL: InterVarsity, 2014.

Spickard, James V. *Alternative Sociologies of Religion: Through Non-Western Eyes*. New York: New York University Press, 2017.

Stanley, Brian. "The World Missionary Conference, Edinburgh 1910: Sifting History from Myth." *The Expository Times* 121 (2010) 325–31.

State Department for Youth. "Kenya Youth Development Policy 2019." https://www.prb.org/wp-content/uploads/2020/06/Kenya-Youth-Development-Policy-2019.pdf.

Strong, Philippa. "Effective Youth Ministry: Theology-Driven in a Cultural Context." *In die Skriflig* 49 (2015) 1–9. https://indieskriflig.org.za/index.php/skriflig/article/view/1889/3103.

Stuart-Buttle, Ross, and John Shortt, eds. *Christian Faith, Formation, and Education*. New York: Springer, 2017.

Sudarkasa, Niara. "The Status of Women in Indigenous African Societies." *Feminist Studies* 12 (1986) 91–103.

Szerszynski, Bronislaw. "Understanding Creationism and Evolution in America and Europe." In *Science and Religion: New Historical Perspectives*, edited by Thomas Dixon et al., 153–74. Cambridge: Cambridge University Press, 2010.

Taylor, Charles. *A Secular Age*. Cambridge: Harvard University Press, 2017.

Tenai, Noah K. "An Enquiry on Poverty Discourses in Public Theology for the Calling of the Church to Respond to Poverty: A Case for the Africa Inland Church in Kenya." *In die Skriflig* 50 (2016) 1–8.

Thomas, Renny. "Atheism and Unbelief Among Indian Scientists: Towards an Anthropology of Atheism(s)." *Society and Culture in South Asia* 3 (2017) 45–67.

Torabi, Maryamossadat, and Seyed Masoud Noori. "Religious Leaders and the Environmental Crisis: Using Knowledge and Social Influence to Counteract Climate Change." *The Ecumenical Review* 71 (2019) 344–55.

Toren, Benno van den. "Researching African Lived Theology: The Value of Non-Traditional Sources in Contextual and Intercultural Theology." African Theology Research Guide, Feb. 26, 2021. https://african.theologyworldwide.com/research-guide/23-researching-african-lived-theology.

Tshaka, Rothney S. "On Being African and Reformed? Towards an African Reformed Theology Enthused by an Interlocution of Those on the Margins of Society." *HTS: Theological Studies* 70 (2014) 1–7.

Twenge, Jean M. *iGen: Why Today's Super-Connected Kids Are Growing Up Less Rebellious, More Tolerant, Less Happy—and Completely Unprepared for Adulthood—and What That Means for the Rest of Us*. New York: Simon and Schuster, 2017.

Ugor, Paul Ushang. "Extenuating Circumstances: African Youth and Social Agency in a Late-Modern World." *Postcolonial Text* 8 (2013) 1–12.

United Nations. "United Nations and Partners Call for $472.6 Million to Respond in 2023 as the Drought in Kenya Deepens." United Nations Kenya, Nov. 21, 2022. https://kenya.un.org/en/208262-united-nations-and-partners-call-4726-million-respond-2023-drought-kenya-deepens.

Van der Ven, Johannes A. *Practical Theology: An Empirical Approach*. Leuven: Peeters, 1998.

Vanhoozer, Kevin J., and Daniel J. Treier. *Theology and the Mirror of Scripture: A Mere Evangelical Account*. Downers Grove, IL: InterVarsity, 2015.

Bibliography

Verhoef, Anné H., and Mark Rathbone. "Economic Justice and Prophetic Discourse in the South African Context—Towards a Dialogical Mode of Discourse." *Journal of Theology for Southern Africa* 145 (2013) 92–109.

Vorster, Jakobus M. "Marriage and Family in View of the Doctrine of the Covenant." *HTS Teologiese Studies/Theological Studies* 72 (2016) 1–8. https://hts.org.za/index.php/hts/article/view/3218.

Ward, Graham. "Decolonizing Theology." *Stellenbosch Theological Journal* 3 (2017) 561–84.

Ward, Peter. *Growing up Evangelical: Youthwork and the Making of a Subculture* 2nd ed. Eugene, OR: Wipf & Stock, 2013.

———. *Growing Up Evangelical: Youthwork and the Making of a Subculture*. London: SPCK, 1996.

———. *Introducing Practical Theology: Mission, Ministry and the Life of the Church*. Grand Rapids: Baker Academic, 2017.

Watkins, Claire. "Qualitative Research in Theology: A Spiritual Turn?" In *The Wiley Blackwell Companion to Theology and Qualitative Research*, edited by Pete Ward and Knut Tveitereid, 16–26. New York: Wiley & Sons, 2022.

Weber, Shantelle. "Decolonising Youth Ministry Models? Challenges and Opportunities in Africa." *HTS Teologiese Studies/Theological Studies* 73 (2017) 1–10. https://doi.org/10.4102/hts.v73i4.4796.

———. "Faith Formation of Young People in an Evangelical Context: An Empirical and Theoretical Investigation." PhD diss, Stellenbosch University, 2014.

———. "A (South) African Voice on Youth Ministry Research: Powerful or Powerless?" *HTS Teologiese Studies/Theological Studies* 71 (2015) 1–6. http://dx.doi.org/10.4102/hts.v71i2.2973.

Weber, Shantelle, and Brandon Weber. "'In the Beginning God Created the Heavens and the Earth': What Do Science and Faith Have to Do With Youth Ministry?" *HTS Teologiese Studies/Theological Studies* 77 (2021) 1–11. https://doi.org/10.4102/hts.v77i2.6834.

Wells, David F. *No Place for Truth: Or Whatever Happened to Evangelical Theology?* Grand Rapids: Eerdmans, 1993.

Wepener, Casparus J., et al. "The Tradition of Practical Theology at the University of Pretoria." *Verbum et Ecclesia* 38 (2017) 133–302.

Westhuizen, Henco van der. "Who Is Christ for Us Today? Bonhoeffer's Question for the Church." *Acta Theologica* 37 (2017) 143–67. http://dx.doi.org/10.18820/23099089/actat.v37i2.9.

Westminster Confession of Faith. Edinburgh: Banner of Truth, 2018.

Wilhoit, James C. *Spiritual Formation as If the Church Mattered: Growing in Christ Through Community*. Grand Rapids: Baker Academic, 2008.

Willard, Dallas. *The Divine Conspiracy: Rediscovering Our Hidden Life in God*. New York: Harper, 1998.

Wimberly, Anne E. Streaty, and Evelyn L. Parker, eds. *In Search of Wisdom: Faith Formation in the Black Church*. Nashville: Abingdon, 2011.

Wimberly, Edward P. *African American Pastoral Care*. Rev. ed. Nashville: Abingdon, 2010.

Woo, Eun-Jung, and Eungoo Kang. "Environmental Issues as an Indispensable Aspect of Sustainable Leadership." *Sustainability* 12 (2020) 1–22.

Bibliography

World Alliance of Reformed Churches. "The Accra Confession: Covenanting for Justice in the Economy and in the Earth." World Communion of Reformed Churches, 2004. https://wcrc.eu/wp-content/uploads/2022/03/AccraConfession-Introduction.pdf.

World Communion of Reformed Churches. "Grape Pilot Project Launched in Africa." Aug. 9, 2022. https://wcrc.eu/grape-pilot-project-launched-in-africa/.

World Economic Forum. "World Economic Forum on Africa: Connecting Africa's Resources Through Digital Transformation." https://www3.weforum.org/docs/WEF_AF16_Report_.pdf.

Yaconelli, Mark. *Contemplative Youth Ministry: Practicing the Presence of Jesus*. Grand Rapids: Zondervan, 2006.

Yoon, Sunny. "Tuning in Sacred: Youth Culture and Contemporary Christian Music." *International Review of the Aesthetics and Sociology of Music* 47 (2016) 315–42.

Young, Shawn David. "Evangelical Youth Culture: Christian Music and the Political." *Religion Compass* 6 (2012) 323–38.

Zuckerman, Phil, et al. *The Nonreligious: Understanding Secular People and Societies*. Oxford: Oxford University Press, 2016.

Zurlo, Gina A., et al. "World Christianity and Mission 2020: Ongoing Shift to the Global South." *International Bulletin of Mission Research* 44 (2020) 8–19.

www.ingramcontent.com/pod-product-compliance
Lightning Source LLC
Chambersburg PA
CBHW051936160426
43198CB00013B/2180